NEWCASTLE MEMORIES

The publishers would like to thank the following companies for their support in the production of this book

Main Sponsor

Newcastle & Whitley Housing Trust

BAE SYSTEMS, RO Defence, Birtley

Bewley & Scott Ltd

Bowey Group Ltd

Chameleon Mirrors

M I Dickson

Eldon Square Shopping Centre

A E Fletcher (Electricals) Ltd

Kavli Limited

Komatsu UK Ltd

John Lewis

Miller UK

Mott MacDonald

Robert Muckle

Murray Hogg

Newcastle Building Society

Newcastle City Council - Grainger Market

Newcastle Libraries

North Eastern Co-op

Northern Electric

Pumphreys Coffee

Stephenson Clarke Shipping Ltd

Storey Sons & Parker

The Travel Bureau Gosforth

Victor Products Ltd

First published in Great Britain by True North Books Limited
England HX3 6AE
01422 344344

ISBN 1 903204 71 2

Text, design and origination by True North Books Limited
Printed and bound by The Amadeus Press Limited

NEWCASTLE MEMORIES

Contents

Introduction

Reading through 'Newcastle Memories' will be a nostalgic journey back to the middle of the last century. That period of modern history is recent enough for some of us to recall and for others to have been told about it by their parents. Yet, it is still irritatingly far enough away for some of the edges to have become blurred and definitive recollections to be uncertain. That is where this publication can help because it draws together some of the memorable moments and stunning sights of the middle of the 20th century and presents them in an attractive and thought provoking manner. Each lovely photograph is accompanied by text that is meant both to inform and to inspire discussion and even argument. The book is not meant to be a dry and dusty revisiting of 50-year old facts, but a gentle trip down memory lane when everything seemed so different and many of the good old days were just that. Not everything in the old garden of remembrance was rosy, of course, because we only have to think of the wartime years when camaraderie mixed with carnage to realise that. Yet, we can be sure that the pace of life and the pressures we faced were not the same as they are now. Newcastle, of course, has a long history stretching way back before the period with which this book deals and we need to reflect briefly upon it to appreciate how those years of development made Geordieland and its people so special. The Romans appreciated the military value of the area when they built their fort and bridge, Pons Aelius, in c122 AD on the Tyne as part of the defence system of Hadrian's Wall. After they left the Saxons settled in the area, but it is with the coming of the Normans that the real development of the town began. William the Conqueror's son, Robert, built a wooden fort, the first 'New Castle', in 1080. The Keep dates from the 12th century and the Black Gate from 1247, with the town walls appearing in the 13th and 14th centuries. Partly thanks to its fortified protections, Newcastle became an important trading centre in medieval times, dealing in such commodities as wool, cloth, fish and hides. The first mayor was appointed in 1216 and, in 1400, the town became a

county borough in its own right. In Tudor times Newcastle was heavily involved in the exporting of coal and, having control of the river, it was able to handle coal mined both locally and further afield, thus increasing the town's revenue.

During the Civil War, Newcastle was under siege for three months in 1644, but soon bounced back to become the next most populated provincial town after Norwich, York and Bristol. In 1724 Daniel Defoe described Newcastle as 'a spacious, extended, infinitely populous place'. That last pair of words hinted at some of the squalor and poverty in older parts of the town which were always the sad corollary to wealth everywhere. It was something that stayed with us, for a report on the sanitary condition of Newcastle published over 100 years later commented that '...some rooms are occupied by 15 to 20 persons each and...those attacked by fever in many cases die and the beds are the very next night occupied again.' Those who did prosper were involved in coal production and shipbuilding and repairing, along with the other heavy industries that blossomed during the industrial revolution. Locomotive building, armaments manufacture and the development of steam turbines were just some of the activities that flourished.

The modern face of our city took shape in the first half of the 19th century, largely thanks to the creativity and imagination of developer Richard Grainger and the architect John Dobson who were able to mould the face of the centre thanks to the inspirational town clerk John Clayton. Many of our large department stores, theatres, fine houses and colleges date from this era. By the time of the 1851 census Newcastle was home to over 87,000 people and, by the time of the first world war, had expanded rapidly to nearly 270,000. The Great War signalled the beginning of the end for many of the industries that had made Newcastle wealthy. Coal, chemicals, engineering and shipbuilding started to face a decline as the depression of the interwar years began to bite. It is from that point in the formal history of Newcastle that 'Newcastle Memories' takes over, not with a further history lesson, but with a poignant eye to the recent past where readers are nudged towards drawing their own conclusions from

the images presented to them and the words accompanying those pictures that are meant to provoke comment and consideration. Visitors to Newcastle are about to discover that there is more to the city than brown ale, the Toon army and six great bridges. Locals will recognise places and buildings, as well as perhaps a few faces, as they once were or as our parents described them. In some situations things might not appear quite how we remembered them, such are the tricks that the memory can play. We are nearly at the start of our voyage into that Aladdin's cave of nostalgia, in the same way that we are nearly in Newcastle when first glimpsing Anthony Gormley's Angel of the North as we drive up the A1.

Let us now go back to an era when people walked on grass rather than smoked it, and when offering your seat on a bus to a pretty girl did not get the response, 'What are you after, then?' Return to the days when apples were bought by the pound from a greengrocer and not by the kilo in a supermarket tray encased in polythene. Fifty years or so ago we walked half a mile to school, not a kilometre in a four-by-four, and said, 'Good morning, sir' to the headmaster, not 'Hiya' to the headteacher. Doctors made house calls without a grumble, shop assistants thanked you for your custom and Cliff Richard was still on the horizon, even if only just. Trains ran on time, bobbies patrolled the streets and motor cars were welcome in the city centre. 'Come on Timmy' was a cry to a dog in Enid Blyton's 'Famous Five', not an exhortation to a tennis player at Wimbledon, and children spoke when they were spoken to and not before. Chips were for putting salt and vinegar on, not for putting into computers, and pubs had waiters who would bring round after round of drinks to your table and expect to be tipped just once in the evening. Women were not ashamed to be housewives and took a pride in knitting jumpers or running up curtains. When was the last time you darned a sock?

But, that is enough of indulging in written memories. Now turn the first page into this treasure trove of photographs where each one is worth a thousand words. Get in the mood by sucking a Spangle, smoking a Craven A and winding up the gramophone to listen to Anne Shelton singing 'Lay down your arms'. As they say in modern restaurants, 'Enjoy'.

Street Scenes

This general view of Newcastle Quayside was taken from across the water above Gateshead in 1950. Among many other notable buildings, the 1929 Salvation Army Men's Palace can be seen next to All Saints' Church. This place of worship, designed by David Stephenson, replaced All Hallows in 1780. Almost unique in its oval shape, the church was deconsecrated in 1961, a comment on the decline in fortunes of this part of Newcastle in those days. The building was converted into offices ion 1984 and partly used as a school resource centre. The Quayside is the oldest part of the city and was once the keystone of its commercial activity. Until the major 19th century building works got under way, the castle keep and the 14th century St Nicholas' Church, and from 1882 the Cathedral, with its distinctive lantern tower, were the major landmarks in the area. In more modern times, regeneration along here has returned the Quayside to a position as one of the focal points of Newcastle activity. Bars, clubs, theatres and cosmopolitan restaurants have revitalised it into a buzzing centre once more. Traditionalists also enjoy an open market that is mounted here every Sunday, with its wide array of goods on sale.

Below: The photograph from the 1950s shows the Darn Crook Co-op to the left, with a view leading away towards Chinatown. This is a decade often ignored by historians and lovers of nostalgia who seem hell bent on reliving the swinging 60s, the flower power 70s or returning to the wartime years for their reminiscing. It is a little like the 'o' in Czechoslovakia that suddenly disappeared when the Czech Republic and Slovakia came into being. It once existed, but now seems to be overlooked. The 50s, after all, was the period when we reconstructed both our bomb damaged buildings and the economy. In 1950 we still had rationing, bombsites and a pound that had just been devalued by 30 per cent. There was also a Labour government in power that had introduced the welfare state and nationalised everything in sight without improving the daily lot of Joe Public. The England football team was embarrassingly beaten in the World Cup by American no-hopers and 'I've got a lovely bunch of coconuts' was the best song we could come up with. Yet, by the time the last day of 1959 came along the shops were full of consumer goods, new housing estates had been built and we had money in our pockets. The Tories had balanced the books, local lad Bobby Charlton was in the national soccer team and BMC had unveiled its Mini motor car. However, Lonnie Donegan was just about to record 'My old man's a dustman', so not everything was for the better. Even so, let's hear it for the 50s.

Above: Newcastle Town Hall, seen on 30 August 1950, was not the most popular of the buildings that appeared in the city centre during the great architectural developments of the mid 19th century. Victorians felt it lacked the grandeur that should be possessed by the focal centre of local government. Keen on ornate design, many offered the view that it was too plain. That opinion might have

caused an eyebrow or two to raise amongst the 1960s' architects who believed in straight, rectangular lines, but our forefathers probably had a point when comparing this building with some of those form the same era. Another objection to its presence, led by the mighty Richard Grainger, complained that the town hall blocked off the view of St Nicholas' church. When it was built at the bottom of Bigg Market in 1858-63, incorporating the Corn Exchange, at a cost of £50,000, little did the architects realise that it would be greeted with such a snooty response. To those of us brought up on concrete slabs and girders it has an imposing and stately look, but each to his own. Aesthetic appreciation will never have uniformity, but perhaps it is a good thing for else we would have completely interchangeable and characterless town centres and that would never do.

H.SAMUEL
BOVRIL

Left: This fine photograph was taken late one afternoon in June 1953, the year in which the whole of whole of Britain and its Commonwealth would celebrate the coronation of its young Queen Elizabeth II in Westminster Abbey. Memories of the second world war are still fresh, but the pain is beginning to fade. Winston Churchill is Prime Minister for a second time and we have just entered the New Elizabethan Age.Here at the junction of Blackett Street and Northumberland Street is a scene of semi-chaos. Almost every make of motor car that might be seen in post war Newcastle can be found here in this delightful snapshot. Trolley buses are also featured, along with a No 26 diesel double-decker seen in the foreground on its way to Pelaw.In the top left hand corner of the picture is the large and very distinctive Burton's Building. This was a monument to the success of the company's founder Montague Burton and his tailoring organisation which had similar (though generally smaller) stores on almost every high street in the country. Is there any man old enough to remember this scene who didn't buy a suit at Burton's?

Below: By 8 January 1953 Philipson and Son had established new premises on Oxford Street that once ran from New Bridge Street to Ellison Place, before the creation of John Dobson Street and other developments altered the face of this part of the city. A small section of the old street still exists, tucked away behind the Laing art gallery and museum. As the year began Philipson's must have looked forward to plenty of promising business in the months to come, culminating in the coronation events that June. There would be plenty of individuals and companies looking for mementoes of the celebrations and those with a keen eye for an opportunity were able to utilise their skills in producing brochures, photographs and prints that would make treasured keepsakes. There were also many other notable events to be recorded during the first half of 1953. Floods devastated the east coast, Stanley Matthews got a winner's medal in the FA Cup Final at last and Everest was conquered. It was Tensing who was alongside Hilary, rather than Philipson's, but the company was still able to contribute to more local historic happenings. Now operating as the Ward Philipson Group it is still a private company, but has grown significantly from its origins as a small firm of printers at the turn of the 19th century and now has premises at Dunston, Newcastle's Percy Street and Gateshead's Metrocentre. The MD, John A Moreels, was awarded the MBE in 1999 for services to small businesses.

Below: Hello playmates! This was a little man with a great standing in the field of British comedy. Arthur Askey, or 'big hearted Arthur' as he was often billed, packed them in wherever he went. When Tate's Radio Company decided to publicise its Shields Road branch it was guaranteed a large turnout by hiring the services of the Liverpuddlian who was a true star of radio, television and the silver screen. You only have to glance at the faces of the crowd and take in the grin of the bobby to know that Arthur was on top form on 15 October 1956. With a line in quick patter and the ability to launch into any of a number of silly songs, such as the one about a busy bee, he had an audience in the palm of his hand in an instant. A dapper little dresser, Askey had no need of clown type costumes to get across the message that he was a funny man. His script and quick wit did that for him. Born in 1900, Arthur joined a concert party in 1924 and started touring the variety halls. His break into the big time came when he was a wow on radio's Band Wagon, ensuring that he headlined shows on stage and on radio until it became time for him to try his hand at television. His golden touch continued and the 1950s' programme 'Before your very eyes' was an enormous success. It also introduced audiences to Norma Sykes, the archetypal dumb blonde Sabrina who could not act, sing, dance or do anything other than look great. Arthur worked well into his 70s and sadly passed away in 1982. As he might have said for us, 'I thank you'.

Right: First time visitors to the north east's premier city are taken aback at their first sighting of Grey's monument. Locals have become quite blase about it, familiarity and all that, but it comes as a real eye opener to any stranger. Standing 135 feet high and enclosing 164 internal steps, its towering presence dominates the surrounding Grey Street, Blackett Street and Grainger Street junction. Seen here in 1956, long before the new Metro underground station was conceived, the monument was erected in 1838. The 13 foot statue, designed by EH Baily, was shipped here from London and winched into place as a salute to Charles, Earl Grey (1764-1845), the prime minister who presided over the passage of the Reform Act of 1832, modernising the franchise and electoral system. Born in Howick, Grey was educated at Eton and Cambridge before entering Parliament as MP for Northumberland at the tender age of 22. In concert with a group of similar thinkers he formed the Society of the Friends of the People in 1792 to encourage lower and middle class demands for parliamentary reform. This was a radical move for the times that won him few friends but gained the respect of many for sticking to his principles. In 1794 Grey married Mary Ponsonby, eventually producing some 15 children, and, despite the demands of family life, went on to the highest political office when he succeeded the Duke of Wellington in 1830.

This breathtaking picture was taken from Grey's monument and shows the handsome sweep of Grey Street, giving a glorious view of the stunning architecture that is the pride of Newcastle. Its beauty and grandeur are acknowledged worldwide, and, from the evidence of the photograph taken in 1957, it is not hard to see the reason why. Lloyd's Bank, formerly the Northumberland and District Bank, the building in the foreground, has corner bays that were once private houses used by bank officials, tellers and clerks. The building's exterior was renovated in the 1980s and the interior remodelled. To the left of centre we can see the Theatre Royal. The first building to have this name was designed by David Stephenson and erected in 1788 on Mosley Street, whereas our present theatre dates from just before Queen Victoria came to the throne. Constructed by John and Benjamin Green, the Theatre Royal opened on 20 February 1837 with a production of 'The Merchant of Venice'. Perhaps someone mentioned the name 'Macbeth' in 1899 because misfortune struck the theatre when it was badly damaged by fire following a performance of 'the Scottish play'. It reopened in 1901 and, apart from a two year closure for restoration in 1986, has continued to present a cultural face to the world, in keeping with the majesty of Grey Street.

Above: For more than 70 years Northumberland Street has succeeded in attracting the most famous retail names, and in the process rightly earning itself the title of the most important shopping street in Britain outside of London. Taken in 1958, this photograph shows Northumberland Street back in the days when electric cables for the trolley bus service criss-crossed the air above our heads. Unlike diesel-engined buses the efficient electrically powered trolley busses didn't spew out vast clouds of choking blue smoke; even so, in the late 1950s, the air was still filled with exhaust fumes from the thousands of motor vehicles which passed along this busy bottleneck in the days before pedestrianisation.The right hand side of the picture is dominated by Pearl Assurance Buildings which once stood at the corner of Northumberland Street and New Bridge Street. Like many fine local buildings this one too was demolished in the 1960s. The spot was known as Cooks Corner by many locals because of the Thomas Cooks travel agents which was located on the ground floor of Pearl Assurance Buildings, and which can be clearly seen here. Many other towns and cities have Pearl Assurance Buildings; they often remind people of theatres built around the same time. Built between 1902 and 1904 the seven storey Pearl Assurance Buildings was designed by one William Hope. And Hope was in fact a nationally renowned theatre designer.

Below: The elevated view along Blackett Street gives an interesting look at the contrast between old and new. Down below is the modern traffic, weaving in and out of lanes, and road markings, such as box junctions, laid down in an effort to keep everything on the move. The delightful architecture of the buildings enhances the panorama, though those responsible for the demolition of the YMCA building in order to create space for the Eldon Square Shopping Centre could not have thought so. It used to be said that a sophisticated person was one who could listen to the 'William Tell Overture' without thinking of 'The Lone Ranger'. In more recent times the same description could be given to someone who saw the YMCA without conjuring up images of a pop group containing men in fancy dress singing a disco song to the accompaniment of silly arm actions. Newcastle's YMCA was built in 1896 and officially opened by Arthur, Duke of Connaught, Queen Victoria's third son, on 10 May 1900. It was a major venture as this building at the junction of Blackett Street, Grainger Street and Grey Street had a 1,000 capacity and included a games room, reading room and gymnasium. Pictured in March 1966, Blackett Street took its name from a family of wealthy landowners involved with smelt mills, refineries and the exporting of lead and silver goods.

Above: The quintet of little scallywags by the old tobacconist's in Elswick on 1 April 1960 might be forgiven for thinking that someone had played an April Fools' Day joke on the neighbourhood that they knew as home. All around them the devastation of the developers was in evidence. In truth, it was not before time for some of the properties in this vicinity. They had long outlived their usefulness and had become classed as slums many years before. Tell that to the lads, though, and you might have got a different reaction. After all, this is the area where they had been brought up and their homes were loving ones, even if the bricks and mortar were crumbling, the outside toilets archaic and the wallpaper damp in places. Elswick owed its origins to William Armstrong, later Baron Armstrong of Cragside, who bought a five acre site here in the middle of the 19th century to build a new engineering works to manufacture hydraulic cranes. His workers and those employed at the shipyard lived in terraced housing along the slopes of the river banks. Armstrong also lent assistance to the British Army, improving the design and manufacture of guns. In the 20th century Elswick became an important centre in the building of such ordnance as tanks and howitzers. Perhaps some of the latter could have been used to blast away the worn out parts of Elswick that still had too many substandard houses even in the 1970s. At last, nearly all have now gone, along with many famous Scotswood Road pubs.

Below: The Royal Arcade on Manor Street was demolished in1963, some 130 years since Richard Grainger built it, probably to John Dobson's design. It was very fashionable in its day and compared well with similar ventures in London and other great regional centres. Containing shops, banks, offices and a steam bath, it was an advanced concept in the days before we entered the Victorian age. The Royal Arcade made way for the construction of Swan House and the mammoth roundabout that now dominates this spot and links with the city motorway, the A167M. Buemann and Riley Brothers, provisions' importers at 1-5 Manor Street, occupied the premises to the right on 29 April 1958. Further right were the stores of Northumberland Hotels Ltd and then William Shaw, a tile layer had his base. Pilgrim Street runs at the side of the Royal Arcade, with Alderman Fenwick's House just out of shot on the left. Despite being a fine building with an imaginatively styled interior, the Royal Arcade was seldom well patronised by ordinary shoppers as it was just that little bit too far out of the city centre. Its rear entrance opened onto Manor Chare, not one of the choicest spots in the area, and this provided another reason for people to steer clear.

At Leisure

Below: George Robey (1869-1954), 'the prime minister of mirth', was one of the seminal figures of the music halls. Unlike most of his contemporaries, he had a middle class upbringing and attended the universities of Leipzig and Cambridge. George entered show business by performing as a mesmerist's assistant at the Westminster Aquarium. He worked his way up the variety ladder, initially as a singer, and widened his repertoire increasingly to include the comedy sketches that earned him his nickname. Robey's stage talents made him a great pantomime dame and, in later years, more prestigious roles in Shakespearean productions and comic opera. On 24 June 1930 he posed for a promotional picture with the boxer, Len Johnson, 'the man they could not knock down'. Len had been to Newcastle three years earlier when he defeated the American, Jack 'Black Dynamite' Walker. Johnson honed his boxing skills in the fairground booths up and down the country and was one of our top fighters, but was denied a title shot while in his prime because of an unofficial colour bar that prevented black boxers getting true recognition. By the time he got his chance, Len was past his best and lost his bout against Len Harvey. Johnson was also unpopular with the powers that be because of his support of the Communist Party in his home town of Manchester. George Robey was knighted for his work, but Len Johnson slipped away into obscurity.

Below: In 1938 the Eldon Building was one of the top spots in the city. Barry Noble's jewellery displays stood out, along with Reed's clock, to the left, but pride of place belonged to the Eldon Grill. Owned by FM Laing and Company Ltd and regarded as Newcastle's most prestigious restaurant, this was where the smart set went to wine and dine. Cosseted by the head waiter and a sommelier suggesting the priciest of wines, guests were assured of the finest cuisine and hospitality. Over the after dinner coffee and brandy, informed talk turned to current affairs. What did those diners make of the situation in Europe, we wonder? How did they view Neville Chamberlain's performance in Munich when he met Herr Hitler and returned home brandishing a little piece of paper that he assured us meant 'peace for our time'? Opinion would have been divided as two distinct camps formed into those who agreed with the policy of appeasement and those who sided with Mr Churchill and doubted the Fuhrer's sincerity. It did not take long for the truth to become clear, because a matter of weeks after the prime minister's hopes for stability were expressed German tanks rolled into Czechoslovakia and the storm clouds over Europe grew blacker than ever.

Below: St George has been slaying the dragon in Eldon Square for longer than he cares to remember. It is we who are the ones who need to recall what he stands for as CI Hartwell designed the bronze statue as a memorial to those who fell in the two world wars. St George, the patron saint of the Northumberland Fusiliers, sits in the square completed by Grainger in 1826. It was named for one of the royal Grammar School's famous old boys, John Scott, Earl of Eldon and Lord High Chancellor of England for most of the period 1801-27. He resigned his post in protest against the Catholic Emancipation plan of the prime minister, George Canning. He must have turned in his grave in 2003 when he learned that another prime minister considered scrapping the post of Chancellor. Nor would he have slept easy when the backdrop to this 1956 scene was replaced by the institutional facade of the Eldon Shopping Centre, looking like something out of 'Cell Block H'. Although the square still attracts people to sit on the grass in the summer sun, even that is tattier than it was half a century earlier when the sward was better cared for and did not suffer from ugly bald patches that blight it today.

Below, large picture: Newcastle played host to the Royal Agricultural Show in 1956 before it eventually found a permanent home in the Midlands. In keeping with its title, notable visitors included the Duke of Northumberland and Queen Elizabeth, the late Queen Mother. This general view inside the grounds shows some of the trade stands with occupiers as diverse as Calor Gas and purveyors of sheep dips. Elsewhere, signs for bee-keeping demonstrations and flower displays capture the rural spirit of the occasion. Within the show there were parades of cattle and horseflesh, all competing to win rosettes within their respective categories. Large marquees offered the opportunity to view exhibitions of country crafts or the chance to sit down to a refreshing cup of tea. The whole environment hummed with activity and the strong animal aromas of the countryside. Riders demonstrated their equestrian skills in the show ring and sheepdogs were put through their paces to the accompaniment of piercing whistles and calls from their owners. Country squires rubbed shoulders with townies as the two life styles came together to enjoy the occasion that gave a flavour of the work of a sector of the community that still existed in our green and pleasant land. There were even prizes for displays of vegetables where allotment holders could compete with the most up to date of farmers. In the background fairground rides buzzed with the excited voices of young children having a whale of a time.

Below: Fenwick's swimming club at the Northumberland Baths was an opportunity for workmates and their families to enjoy a few lengths of the pool as a break from the rigours of the daily grind. This 1950s' photograph suggests that this was a more organised occasion than usual as a race seems to be taking place. Women nearly always wore swimming caps, not to improve their aerodynamic lines through the water, but simply to keep their hair dry. Electric hair dryers were not part of their normal bedroom equipment and expensively permed hair needed protection. It was also a statement of modesty as women did not like to be seen out and about without some sort of headwear, though this seems a little ridiculous considering that they were baring other parts of their anatomy without a care in the world. On practice days the girls imagined that they were Esther Williams in some glamorous Hollywood spectacular and the boys pretended to be Buster Crabbe or some other Olympic champion. The public baths were built in 1838 at Ridley Place, on the east side of Northumberland Street, occupying an area of 172 by 132 feet. Costing £9,500 to build to a design by John Dobson, the baths were originally advertised as having warm shower, vapour, tepid medication and plunge baths. They were intended for use by the poor in an effort to improve hygiene and it was thought that the lower classes would spend more leisure time in them rather than on the streets or in public houses.

Above: All the fun of the fair, and sports day as well. This was the annual bash for Hedley's employees and families as they enjoyed themselves in the open air. Thomas Hedley, the soap manufacturer, was not content to build an empire. He also looked to put something back into his local community. To this end he served on the town council, becoming chairman of the finance committee for a long period in the middle of the 19th century. Hedley was also a director and chairman of the Newcastle and Gateshead Gas Company. It was in keeping with his interest in others that the company organised the fun of this sports day on 4 July 1953. It was one of those rare occasions when everything seemed right about British sport. Gordon Richards had his Derby winner at long last when Pinza shot past the post, Denis Compton helped regain the Ashes from the Aussies and the Cup Final was a seven-goal thriller as Blackpool came back from the dead to pip Bolton in the every last minute when Bill Perry converted a Stan Matthews cross. The lady in the photograph trying to score a goal pretended that she was Stan Mortenson, the centre forward who notched a hat trick at Wembley. We can only hope that her contact with the ball was minimal in those shoes or the St John's Ambulance might have got a call.

Top right: What simple pleasures we had at the start of the swinging 60s and, as children, so many of them were to be had in the local park. We played on the swings, got giddy spinning on the roundabouts and came down to earth with a bump on the seesaw. There were endless games of cricket on the grass or massive games of soccer when a pair of coats made do as goalposts. There were bushes where we could play hide and seek and plenty of opportunity to turn a skipping rope, shouting, 'Salt, mustard, vinegar, pepper.' Paddling pools and lakes gave us a chance to sail little home-made boats that invariably twirled round and sank and there was always the chance that Auntie Florrie would lose her footing and get a soaking to make our day complete. The 1870 Improvement Act enabled the town council to develop Town Moor for public use as parkland. Leazes Park opened in 1873, followed by Bull Park and Brandling Park. We can also thank some of our Victorian philanthropists for gifts of land and money that helped provide us with such amenities. The one in the photograph is Paddy (Patrick) Freeman's Park at Jesmond Dene. The chap on the park bench looks amused by the antics of the youngsters by the water. He was probably thinking that they were just like he used to be, getting great fun from simple pursuits.

Right: This was the ideal to which young couples aspired in the Macmillan era. On 31 October 1958, as this pair displayed the very best in materialism, the prime minister's words of the previous year, 'You've never had it so good', still rang loud and true. They had money in the bank, owned their own house and filled it with the latest electrical gadgets. Their parents were amazed to see them with a washing machine, fridge and Richard Greene cavorting as Robin Hood inside a box in a corner of the sitting room, now called a lounge. The young people owned a stylish A40 and had a front lawn to mow instead of a step to donkey-stone. That their daughter in law still taught at the local infant school after her marriage was even more amazing. Whatever next; surely she was not going to learn to drive? The older generation took some time to adjust to the new order, for it was weaned on a diet of economic depression and two world wars. It was not the lot of the working man to have luxuries or takr them for granted and, yet, here were his offspring treating such items as standard fare. Soon, it would be a fortnight in Spain instead of Whitley Bay and a coffee percolator would push the teapot to the back of the cupboard.

There were roundabouts with capsules where little children a decade before could sit and imagine that they were Flash Gordon, swooping down in his rocket and trailing sparks behind him, as he went to do battle with Ming the Merciless. In 1964 they were more up to date and pretended to be Yuri Gagarin or Alan Shepard, those true life pioneers of space. Dodgem cars crashed together and squealing youngsters came whizzing down the helter-skelter on prickly coconut mats. Dads squinted through an off centre sight on the barrel of an air rifle as they tried to hit a metal duck that popped up its head at the back of

the booth. Others tried to dislodge a coconut that seemed impervious to the number of balls that struck it, staying firmly in place while punters muttered something about strong glue. All this took place as the Animals' record, 'Baby let me take you home', belted out over the tannoy. Everyone was enjoying all that the Hoppings had to offer. The event had begun as Town Moor Temperance Festival in 1882 as a counter attraction to the excesses of gambling and drink at Gosforth Park. After a temporary move to Jesmond Vale (1914-23), the Hoppings returned to Town Moor to become established as the world's largest non-permanent fair.

Hands up all those who did their courting on the back row of the ABC Haymarket in July 1966. Younger readers may need to have the word explained to them. Courting was a ritual that couples undertook in the days when boy met girl: they fell in love, got married, lived together and had children, all in that order. Somehow that time table seems now to have been muddled. Back then a girl was asked out for the evening and could expect her young man to buy the tickets for the cinema seats and a box of Payne's Poppets to munch on during the film. On that first date, the more daring beau might hold her hand during the Pearl and Dean adverts, but restrict himself to a modest peck on the cheek after walking her home at the end of the evening. Only on subsequent occasions would anything livelier take place on the double seats at the back of the cinema and, even then, an usherette with a bright beam to her torch made sure that there was only so much hanky and a minimum of panky. As was usually the case, the ABC showed a double feature. 'The Moving Target' starred Paul Newman and Lauren Bacall in the story of a private eye hired to find a rich woman's missing husband. The 'B' movie, 'Kisses for my President', was not a prequel to a tale about Bill Clinton and Monica Lewinsky, but a limp comedy about a woman becoming the President of the USA.

Wartime

Better late than never. Britain finally woke up to the threat posed by Fascist forces on the Continent when Neville Chamberlain's attempts at appeasement were ridiculed by the subsequent German invasion of Czechoslovakia. Civil defence exercises were mounted as the inevitability of war loomed large. Air raid precautions (ARP) were begun and volunteer units began working in earnest in an attempt to get the nation ready to take action in the face of an attack on our homeland. This group practised outside Newcastle Golf Club on 19 February 1939, pretending to mount a rescue from a burning building. Two men in flat caps in the doorway suck thoughtfully on their pipes as they watched the exercise taking place. They noticed that the ARP men had donned gas masks. The fear of chemical warfare was very real, based on evidence from the First World War and accusations levelled at combat forces in the recent Spanish Civil War. In the summer of 1939 some masks were issued to those members of the civilian population living in high risk areas and training classes in their use were hurriedly mounted. Thankfully, no such weapons were used, but the firefighting practice and rescue techniques that the ARP members used served them well when the bombs began falling for real.

Below: Suddenly it was all over. Britain took to the streets to celebrate victory and the desperate days of nearly six years of privation were forgotten, albeit temporarily. On 8 May 1945, and in the following few days, the streets were a riot of colour as bunting, streamers and flags, left over from George VI's coronation, were pulled out of boxes in the loft and flown high with pride. People danced the hokey-cokey and threw street parties where trestle tables were commandeered from church halls and schoolrooms. Someone found a smart tablecloth and another cut flowers to make a smart table decoration. Jealously-guarded rations were raided to provide buns, jellies and sandwiches for the children whose eyes lit up at the array of goodies in front of them. In London, the Royal Family was not allowed to leave the balcony of Buckingham Palace until it had waved yet again to the thousands cheering 'God save the King!" over and over. Licensed premises stayed open all night and servicemen were carried shoulder high through the revellers. Every side street seemed to mirror the scene photographed here. Some of the children were too young to appreciate what was happening, while others wondered what their fathers looked like. It is a sobering thought that not all of them would ever know.

Right: After six long years of mayhem it was with as much relief as rejoicing that we celebrated the end of hostilities once final victory had been assured. Marching bands and endless parades by regular and volunteer forces appeared on our streets as we gave thanks to the brave men and women who had seen us through those dark days. We took to the streets in our thousands and cheered and clapped as we waved the flag to salute our heroines and heroes. Included in the ranks of those in the march past were members of the army that Hitler forgot, those who stayed at home but did their bit, nonetheless. The Women's Voluntary Service, Home Guard, Auxiliary Fire Service, Red Cross, St John Ambulance, Land Army, Auxiliary Territorial Service, Air Raid Precautions and so many more groups deserved our praise as much as those who had taken to the skies, sailed the seas or fought land battles so that Johnny could sleep in his own little room again. When victory was first declared, complete strangers hugged one another and joined in impromptu congas across the city centre. We partied like there was no tomorrow. Sadly, for countless thousands of others this was true, for they had paid the ultimate price in their battle to preserve our freedom. Their sacrifice should never be forgotten and it is important that their memory is kept alive.

THE
METROPOLE
Siesta

Volunteer groups, such as the Women's Voluntary Service, performed a valuable task during World War II. They organised salvage collections, gave instruction on gas mask use and air raid precautions, acted as co-ordinators of rescue missions and went into dangerous situations with their supply vans, providing refreshment for firefighters and ambulance crews with little regard for their own safety as buildings burned and rubble fell around them. This canteen van was one of the first to come into use as a mixture of purpose-built vehicles and converted buses were hurriedly commissioned. Sandbags are just visible in front of the houses in the background. These were not issued until after war broke out as Britain tried to catch up with the precautionary measures overlooked by a blinkered government that acted too late in fully preparing our home defences against attack. The three men from the Auxiliary Fire Service enjoying a warming cuppa in 1940 had joined up in 1937-38. The National Fire Service came into being on 18 August 1941 at a time when the country was under the cosh from seemingly endless waves of enemy bombers that filled the skies over our major cities. The man on the far right is Jack Peer. Happily, he survived the war and was with us until the 1980s. We owe him and his colleagues our thanks for their steadfast displays of courage and professionalism. The identities of the others are unknown, though some readers may be able to recognise a relative to whom we owe an enormous debt. The two men alongside Jack Peer wore World War I service ribbons and did their bit for the country twice over. The one in the middle was obviously the section officer, to judge from his epaulettes.

Events & occasions

Left: In 1935 Northumberland Street was offering its loyal greetings to King George V on the occasion of his silver jubilee, having acceded to the throne on the death of his father, Edward VII on 6 May 1910. George V was a popular monarch who pleased the public when he renounced his family's Germanic name of Saxe-Coburg-Gotha in 1917, replacing it with Windsor. He was also appreciated for his dislike of most things foreign, saying, 'Abroad? Been there once; didn't like it.' The public was glad to celebrate his 25 years on the throne as it had little other reason to party during those days of depression and high unemployment. We can see how busy Northumberland Street had become, even all that long time ago, with cars and trams clogging the road making life difficult for pedestrians. In later years a footbridge was built over the end of Northumberland Street, near to Burton's, the site of the present Monument Mall. To the right was the Queen's Hall, originally intended to be a 2,500 seater concert hall, hotel and 1,000 capacity cinema when plans were unveiled in 1911. This ambitious project was shelved and the smaller cinema built in 1913. On this day, Cicely Courtneidge (1893-1980) was starring in the movie 'Things are Looking Up', an optimistic title in those days for a film that told of a circus horsewoman who has to pose as her schoolmistress sister. Born in Sydney, she played musical comedy and revue, both in a celebrated partnership with her husband, Jack Hulbert, and as a highly talented comedienne in her own right. She became a Dame in 1972.

Below: Ward 19 at Newcastle RVI had been festooned with the obligatory Christmas streamers. On 28 December 1951 those unlucky enough to have spent the festive season under the hospital sheets at least enjoyed some semblance of Yuletide spirit to help lessen the disappointment of separation from the turkey and plum pud at home. A mock-up bar had been donated to the ward, along with the appropriate tipples, to help these bedridden souls endure their stay. The 'ails and whines' were obviously the inspiration of a wag intended to lift their 'spirits', though the Guinness poster was for real. It was one in a long series of witty adverts that have helped the sales of the black nectar over many years. The 'Guinness for strength' slogan was one that also caught the fancy of some of the medical profession. Tuberculosis was a disease still affecting many and doctors often prescribed a daily drink or two of stout as a pick-me-up in the convalescent period after treatment. Patients approved. It was a far better tonic than Sanatogen. Edward VII opened the infirmary on 11 July 1906, six years after he had laid the foundation stone. Built on a ten acre site at Castle Leazes, it was funded partly by subscription, but owed much more to the generosity of philanthropists Hall and Armstrong who each contributed hugely to the cost.

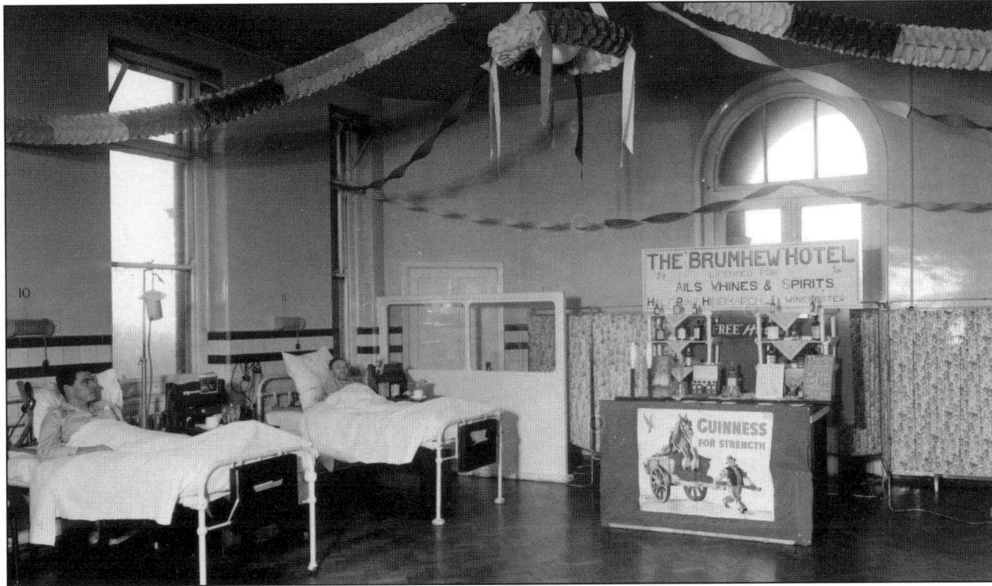

Above: Newcastle's Co-operative Society building in Newgate Street on 31 May 1953 was well prepared for the festivities that would begin a few days later. The Union flags flew proudly from the twin towers and the facade was garlanded with glorious decorations, streamers, flowers and bunting in honour of the great day that was to come. Above the main door the royal coat of arms was handsomely displayed as a tribute to the young queen who was to be crowned in Westminster Abbey on 2 June. When that day dawned there was some disappointment that the sun had not seen fit to shine, but even the rain could not dampen the spirits of the people who lined the streets leading to the Abbey. Those who were there will never forget such sights as the huge frame of Queen Salote of Tonga grinning broadly and waving vigorously as her coach filled with water. We at home gathered round a little television set belonging to a neighbour who discovered that suddenly he was the most popular man in the street. Richard Dimbleby's rich, sonorous tones were perfect in describing the pomp and pageantry and, when Archbishop Fisher lowered the crown onto Queen Elizabeth's head, we joined in the cheers, shouting 'Vivat Regina!', or the Geordie equivalent.

Just two days to go before the Coronation and everything was in place. It looks quiet now, but in 48 hours' time there will be processions, marching bands, a mayoral address and street parties celebrating the day when Elizabeth II was formally blessed as our monarch. She was the youngest person to accede to the throne for over 100 years, that honour being held by her great great-grandmother Victoria. All the major city centre buildings flew flags and were festooned with appropriately coloured decorations. The Northern Gas Board offices were no exception. Standing on Grainger Street, the building's address paid homage to the prolific Richard Grainger (1797-1861). Apprenticed to a builder at the age of 12, he set up on his own before he was out of teenage and soon built a terrace in Higham Place and houses in New Bridge Street, Carliol Street and Blackett Street. When just 28 he embarked on the major project of building Eldon Square, using designs by John Dobson and Thomas Oliver, and completed this task in 1831. By then his influence on Newcastle architecture was well established and he continued to have a great impact on the city centre layout, building the Theatre Royal, Central Exchange, Grey Street, Grainger Street and many more besides.

Watson House stands at the corner of New Bridge Street and Pilgrim Street. The photograph dates from c1950 as the tramlines are still in place. In the distance we can make out Burton's and the YMCA building, while eagle eyes should be able to spot the clock belonging to Northern Goldsmiths on the left. Many of the names on the shops live on today, though not necessarily at the same location. Halford's cycles and Johnson's dry cleaners are just as prominent in the 21st century as they were in the middle of the last one. Over 50 years ago shoppers were looking forward to the start of a new decade that they hoped would bring greater prosperity to their door than had been offered by the 1940s. With typically British optimism, they believed that the next ten years could hardly be worse than those they had endured during the war and its immediate aftermath. Realistically, things were not that rosy. Some goods were still rationed and money was tight as the nation tried to rebuild its economy. There was little spare cash to spare for luxuries such as motor cars, so we used public transport, pedal power or good old Shanks's pony to get around. The Labour government we voted into power in 1945 had yet to deliver its promise of a brave new world.

Shopping spree

Below: Every town has its shops that offer cheaper goods than their bigger named competitors. They are usually given some obvious title that advertises their purpose such as Mr Value, Krazy Kuts or Daft Discounts and are tucked away from the main shopping centres in cheaper-rated outlets. Grahame's on Cross Street was one of that style of shop. The People's Bargain Store had a variety of knick-knacks and items to suit every occasion, including crockery, jewellery, cutlery and what it called 'fancy goods'. To tell from the crowded doorway, Grahame's was a popular place for shoppers to browse around in the hope of spotting something at a knockdown price. Aladdin's jeweller's was sandwiched in between Grahame's shop fronts and its name suggested that it, too, held a treasure trove for those shopping at the bottom end of the market. Wallis and Linnell's wholesale clothier's shop was to the right of Grahame's while, across the way at 23-29 Fenkle Street, the printing firm of John Bowes Ltd can be seen. The warehousemen Campbell, Stewart and McDonald were also based nearby. This pair of streets is still with us, just as tucked away as ever off Westgate Road and Clayton Street, close to the indoor mini-market.

Below: On the right, propped up at the kerb, the delivery boy's bike was a common feature of life half a century ago. A housewife could place an order for groceries and, by the time she was back home from her other shopping, a cheerful lad, whistling a hit tune of the day, would be at the door with a box full of provisions. With a tip of a couple of pence in his pocket he was off back to the Meadow Dairy Company to load up for his next delivery. Trading from 8 Nun Street, this company was listed as a butter dealer, but it also dealt in cooked meats, preserves and other grocery commodities. The first floor was given over to AW Durno and Sons, travelling drapers, while E Lofthouse, a wholesale confectioner and tobacconist, was above 10 Nun Street. Further along, beyond the Nag's Head, were the premises of A Bookless, a fruiterer, and Lockhart and Smith's refreshment rooms. However, on 19 October 1950, pride of place was taken by Farnon's drapery store. John Farnon established his business in 1867 and his successors had helped make his shop a bright and cheerful oasis that stood out amidst the rather forbidding exteriors of its fellow traders. Farnon's display windows were as attractive as some of the others were gloomy.

Bottom right: Percy Street is now a busy, traffic-laden thoroughfare that acts as little more than a means of accessing the shopping centre at Eldon Square or the Haymarket bus station. Its deserted nature on 27 July 1950 is at odds with the scene we would witness here today. There are some shops and bars that trade here, but most of the retail attention has shifted to the core closer to Grey's monument. The ones that were in evidence in this photograph suggest that Percy Street was home to a number of individual, diverse businesses. They included Thompson's, Percy Stores, the Grainger Boot Stores, Kiddie Kot for all your baby and maternity wear, Bower's sandwich shop, Gordon Richmond for your decorating needs, HS Swinden for knives and tools and an antique shop. There was plenty of choice, though these establishments were not the sort that satisfied our daily needs. Percy Street shares its name with that of the Earls of Northumberland whose line was created at Richard II's coronation in 1377, elevating the then Baron Percy of Alnwick to greater status. He and his son Sir Henry Percy, the celebrated Hotspur, are commemorated in William Shakespeare's play Henry IV part I.

Top right: As the young lad made his way along the footpath beside the coastal road he was obviously heading for the tobacconist and sweetshop on his left, rather than the Rising Sun Hotel in the distance that Eric Burdon once sang about; though we might be confusing Newcastle with New Orleans! The youngster's short trousers and baggy socks belong to a form of dress code adopted by all boys of his age in the early summer of 1952. He was not concerned about high fashion and how much would that be worth to modern parents when their children demand the latest in trainers with flashing lights or a black and white replica shirt with 'Dyer' or 'Jenas' emblazoned

on the back? It was also a sign of the times that someone had left a bicycle propped up near to the shop, safe in the knowledge that it would still be there on his return. Do that now and somebody will have pinched the tree as well as the bike before you can blink an eye. What was the youngster going to buy with his pocket money? Would it be some bullseyes, a penny chew, a stick of licorice or a sherbet dip? Maybe he was a reader and was going to get the 'Wizard' and find out if Wilson had run another three minute mile and won the Ashes single handedly yet again. The posters on the gable end seem dated now, with their adverts that included ones for the South Shields' Wright's biscuits, Mitchell's Compass cigarettes and Tide washing powder.

RERS.
NORMAN
GLOVER
& CO.
Benefit
FOOTWEAR
38

Left: Normally, Northumberland Street was thronged with shoppers, but 3 January 1952 had dawned wet and chilly. Only a few intrepid souls ventured out and, in any case, they probably had little left in their purses after funding Christmas. This part of Newcastle, now pedestrianised, has become one of its main shopping areas. Famous names, such as Woolworth's at 15-23 and Fenwick's at 25-39, dominated the 1952 retail scene here. The original five and ten cent store alongside the prestigious court dressmaker, ladies' tailor and furrier provided a balance of shopping opportunity, but there were other smaller enterprises here as well. In the picture we can see Benefit footwear, Thomas Hunter and Jackson's, but there were also the estate agents Glover Norman and Finlay's tobacconist's nearby at no 41. Northumberland Street was formerly largely residential, containing a proliferation of 18th century town houses. It was also popular with marching groups and hosted many demonstrations against the status quo, including the suffragette movement that trod the carriageway on a number of occasions in the early 1900s. Their emancipated successors now have difficulty marching to the shops as they need to weave in and out of the crowds that make Northumberland Street a hive of activity throughout the day.

Below: The Co-op's autumn fashion show was in full swing, but the local population had to settle for something less than might be offered today by Naomi Campbell, Heidi Klum or Claudia Schiffer. Anyway, when did you ever see someone walking down Grey Street dressed in one of those crazy creations that come from the fashion houses of the major European cities? Novocastrians are more practical folk than their southern or continental cousins and even more so on 6 September 1956 when this model made her way down the catwalk. The coat she was wearing was for everyday use and drew admiring glances from the audience in the hall. Calf length was the fashion of the day and something that had been in vogue for a decade when women returned to more feminine styles after the war, tired of utility clothing and necessarily short skirts, given the lack of material available. It would not be until the Mary Quant days of the swinging 60s that hemlines would shoot upwards, giving men palpitations in direct proportion to the amount of leg on display. The women watching the show nearly all wore hats as it was not thought to be ladylike to go out of the house bareheaded. The occasional exception to this unwritten rule, displaying her Toni perm for all to see, was thought to be very daring and even a little risqué.

The Bigg Market area is not a place for the faint hearted these days as it is one of the liveliest centres of nightlife for the young and trendy. With bars being granted liquor licences until the wee, small hours, party goers have a whale of a time in such hot spots as the Yell, Kiss, Bar M, the Vault and the improbably named Blu Bambu. Quite what these shoppers would have made of it in 1958 begets the imagination. They were happy to check the price of fruit and vegetables on the barrows and stalls before deciding upon the purchases that would then find their way into the large shopping bags housewives

always carried. 'Bigg' is probably derived from an old word for 'barley', giving some idea of the commodities that were sold or exchanged around here in days of yore. The banter of the traders and the chat with friends that you bumped into was all part of the fun of being on Bigg Market. The stallholders greeted each customer as if she were a long lost pal or old sweetheart, and she went along with it as it was all goodnatured nonsense. The market, dating back to Norman times, was the city's oldest, but as people dance the night away near here today they will sadly not spare a thought for those days gone by.

Above: The old Green Market, at the top of Nun Street, was piled high with fruit and vegetables that were just that bit more keenly priced than those found in the greengrocers' shops or new supermarkets that had started to appear by August 1966. Housewives looked keenly for a bargain and it was often a good idea to come late in the day and get an even better price as stallholders sold off produce at a cut rate rather than see it go to waste. Fresh food from the farms and market gardens had a more natural taste, even if the carrots were at times oddly shaped and the spuds had the occasional spade cut marking the middle. Sometimes you got more than you bargained or paid for, especially when biting into an apple. There was only one thing worse than discovering a grub in the centre and that was to find half of one! That summer, the men strolling around the market had only one topic of conversation. On 30 July England had won soccer's World Cup, the only major footballing trophy to come the way of our national team before or since that memorable occasion at Wembley. Ashington's own Charlton brothers, Jack and Bobby, were two of the famous team, playing in every match of the tournament that is now a part of sporting legend, along with a very nice Russian linesman.

Above centre: Cookery programmes on television have become big business. It seems that you cannot turn on your set these days without seeing someone with spiky hair, or another waving a picture of a green pepper leering out of the box at you. One of this breed of so-called entertainers was even honoured in the 2003 Queen's birthday list, for goodness sake. Our mums and grannies had no need of wannabe personalities telling them how to prepare recipes. They relied on good old fashioned cookery books and lessons learned at their own mothers' knees. That began to change in the 1950s as the new media of TV took hold. The bearded Philip Harbin was one of the first cookery personalities, but it was the screamingly funny Fanny and Johnny Craddock who really captured the headlines. The hoot of it all was that they were deadly serious and had little idea that they were so hilarious. With Fanny's bossy attitude and Johnny's penchant for unwittting double entendres about his wife's Christian name, they ruled the roost of television cookery in the 60s and 70s. The only real challenge came from across the Atlantic in the shape of Graham Kerr, the galloping gourmet. In our photograph of 17 March 1959 local housewives are being persuaded to celebrate St Patrick's Day with that American idea, the doughnut. Liberal helpings of Trex and the Victoria Flour Company's 'Feathery Flake', plus an investment in a special doughnut machine, were all that was required for success. The housewives enjoyed the demonstration but stuck to their own tried and tested fruit scones.

Who would have thought that the traditional Co-op, founded in a little Lancashire shop on Toad Lane by the Rochdale Pioneers in 1844, was to become another sort of pioneer by 5 March 1958? There was still the divvy to be paid as housewives collected stamps on their cards that they could later exchange, but some blinked in surprise as a shopping revolution hit the Lemington branch of the Blaydon Co-operative Wholesale Society. Self service had arrived. The aping of the American style of shopping did not go down too well with everybody because many missed the personal touch and an opportunity to chat with someone behind the counter. But, others embraced the novelty value and the chance to see what they were buying at closer quarters. It also gave the proprietor the opportunity to do away with the need for the back room where so many items were stored and get much more out on display, hopefully encouraging a greater loosening of the purse strings. Notice how trusting we were in those days. Mum has left the baby in the pram quite happy in the knowledge that no harm will come to her little one. Do-gooders now would be screaming about neglect and sending for the social services to lecture the poor woman about the perils of abduction.

New homes for old

One of the most fundamental needs of every person is a decent home. But until the post war slum clearances and massive building programmes of the period many folk lived in substandard housing without the kind of facilities such as indoor plumbing which are taken for granted today. But if many of us still lived in houses unfit for human habitation until the 1960s things were far worse in earlier times.

Many more of us today own our own homes than used to be the case, but many still prefer, or are obliged, to rent property. Locally one of the largest providers of inexpensive rented flats and houses is the Newcastle and Whitley Housing Trust Ltd, an organisation which sets out to provide affordable homes for those who cannot afford to buy. But things were not always thus.

Above left: *Edith Moffat, 1860-1952, the Social Housing Pioneer.* ***Above right:*** *A share certificate from 1933.* ***Below and right:*** *A sitting room in one of the Trust's homes in the 1950s. In the corner of the room is the 'kitchen cupboard' shown open below.*

Slum landlords of the past expected a 15 per cent return on their money, and that rate was achieved by landlords doing very little to repair their property. Such property could be bought very cheaply because the only buyers were others with the same idea of maximising profit. The very poor were easy victims to such practices and became accustomed to living in dreadful conditions.

The solution to this problem was pointed out by Octavia Hill a Victorian social reformer born in 1838; her remedy was twofold: firstly to buy up bad property using mortgages requiring interest payments of only 4 or 5 per cent; and secondly to train suitable women of 'an intelligent class and make it their pride and purpose after collecting the rents to spend as much of these as possible on the upkeep of property and the welfare of tenants. In 1860 Octavia Hill put her ideas into practice, and using money

NO. OF CERTIFICATE

REGISTERED NO. OF SHAREHOLDER

THE NORTH SHIELDS & TYNEMOUTH HOUSING IMPROVEMENT TRUST LIMITED.

Registered pursuant to the Industrial and Provident Societies Acts, 1893 to 1913, as a Public Utility Society within the meaning of the Housing Acts.

SHARE CERTIFICATE.

This is to Certify that

of

is the registered holder of

of One Pound (£1) each numbered 1 to 100. inclusive. Fully Paid Shares in the above Society, subject to the Rules of the Society.

Given under the Common Seal of the said Society this Seventeenth day of March 1933.

Members of Committee of Management.

Registrar and Secretary.

borrowed from the painter John Ruskin bought a house in London's Nottingham Place. Many more properties would follow.

Thus was born the idea of the housing association: a charitable movement which would have far reaching consequences, not least in Newcastle.

The Newcastle Upon Tyne Housing Improvement Trust was founded in 1928 and became an incorporated body in the following year.

Top left: *Reverand Henry de Candole (pictured right), an early supporter of the work of the Trust.*
Top right: *Reverend Noel Hudson, another supporter of the Trust.* ***Above left:*** *Ruth Buckingham at the opening of Edith Moffat House.* ***Right:*** *Edith Moffat House.*

It is believed that the Trust was formed by a group of philanthropic businessmen after hearing a sermon preached by Ronnie Hall on Christmas Day 1927 at St Luke's Church on the subject of "Homes". Their earlier efforts were later supported by members of the Quaker Church, an unbroken link which still survives into the present day. The earliest surviving records of the Trust are the minute books and press cuttings concerning the first official meeting held on 23rd November 1928.

What is not in doubt is that the Trust has always been a provider of housing - and it still owns one of the first houses it bought for re-letting in Hawthorne Terrace, Elswick.

Originally the Trust operated on a purely voluntary basis. The very first paid member of staff, Miss Agnes Jennings, was appointed in 1929. Agnes Jennings seems to have been involved with Octavia Hill, having worked with her in London before coming to Newcastle. Today, despite massive changes in the following decades, the Trust still only employs some 24 staff.

One local area in particular was a source of deep concern back in the 1920s: the west end of Newcastle, particularly the area between Elswick Road on the north, Scotswood Road to the south, Rye Hill in the east and Beech Grove Road in the west. Built mainly between 1830 and 1880 the area had once been prosperous and contained many large houses, but these were now being sold off by their original owners

and were often roughly converted into flats or tenements. The declining prosperity of the area was well illustrated by the number of barefoot children reported to be seen playing in the streets as well as the number of 'For sale' signs in the locality.

In the autumn of 1930 the Tyneside Council of Social Service, headed by its remarkable Director Dr Henry A Mess, made an enquiry into the extent to which houses originally built for one family were now being occupied by several. The report made grim reading and lead eventually to large-scale slum clearance and to the improvement in living conditions for many thousands of tenement dwellers.

The enquiry found that there were some 2,200 houses in the area, of which almost 900 were occupied by more than one family. A sample of 58 houses which appeared to have multiple occupants was visited. Though some of the houses were quite large it still makes astonishing reading today to discover that more than 600 people were found to be living in those 58 houses, with up to eight people living in a single room. Indeed no fewer than 16 families of five or more people were found to be living in

Right: *George Bowran House, Newcastle.*
Below: *The Trust's Tyneside Flats in Lower Benwell.*

single rooms. In 32 cases the only means of cooking was on an open fire. Of the houses inspected 26 had no indoor water supply. Seventy families had nowhere to wash their clothes whilst 96 families shared a toilet with two or more other families.

The sole exception to this litany of woe was a property owned by the Newcastle Housing Improvement Trust, the forerunner of the Newcastle and Whitley Housing Trust. A key individual in the Trust's past was its first paid employee, Agnes Jennings, a particularly outspoken individual and lady not slow in publicly criticising the effects of poverty and exploitation on the working classes. Such was the success of the Trust in tackling issues of poverty and poor housing conditions, Miss Jennings was seconded to Sunderland Housing Society to lend a hand with her own unique approach to housing management. The working classes were however not universally grateful for her concern: Miss Jennings was showered with sausages and black puddings thrown from houses decorated with kettles and frying pans when she went to collect rents in Sunderland's East End. The cause of all the excitement was Miss Jennings' public pronouncement in the Trust's annual report about the housekeeping standards and methods of cooking practised by working class housewives, remarks which were deeply resented by them. In the Trust's report Miss Jennings had written that 'still another difficulty is that ideas of cooking are bounded by the frying pan. Families consider themselves martyr to poverty on tea, bread and margarine where some knowledge of food values and simple cookery would make less money go further. Sewing seems to be a dying art and a good many of the ragged children one sees everywhere are as they are for want of care. Death insurance money is spent not on necessities for living but on 'black' and the extravagant spread

Top: *The view from the Royal Quays development.* ***Above left:*** *Annitsford.* ***Above right:*** *A wrought iron feature at the Royal Quays.* ***Above:*** *The plaque commemorating the opening of Bicknell House in 1989.*

which tradition demands. Then the annual baby!' Miss Jenning's remarks were all well intended no doubt, but those who were grateful for better homes provided by the Trust and their neighbours were far less grateful for the gratuitous advice on how to sew and cook.

With a length of sausage still wrapped around her neck Miss Jennings was hustled away from the scene by a pair of passing evangelists; bravely she returned later in the day to collect more rents but was booed in the street before making her retreat on a bus.

Above: *A typical Newcastle street scene from the early 20th century.* ***Below:*** *A view of Newcastle from Bicknell House.*

But whatever the views of those being criticised Miss Jennings stuck to her guns and was later stoutly defended by the Reverend RS Bawtree: at the next meeting of the Trust he declared 'Every word of Miss Jennings report can be substantiated. She is the best friend our poor people have had in this kind of work'. Indeed Miss Jennings drew attention to all kinds of problems faced by the poor not least exploitation by money lenders. Many of the poor were slaves to the 'tuppence a bob' system of money lending. A woman who was short of 4 shillings (20p) of her five shillings weekly rent on Monday would go to an unlicensed money lender (who also supplied her with groceries 'on tick' at her own scale of charges) and borrowed the four shillings. On Thursday or Friday, having obtained her unemployment benefit or Parish Relief, she would pay back the four shillings plus 8d (3p) an amount equivalent to an

annual interest rate of over 866 per cent! No wonder folk found it so hard to escape from the poverty trap back then.

Whatever her faults no-one could accuse Miss Jennings of being anything less than plucky and hard working. In recognition of her indomitable spirit and unflagging efforts the trustees awarded her a pay rise in 1930, pushing her salary up to the dizzy heights of £26 a year - or ten shillings (50p) week.

Top: *Tenants and staff from the Trust on their 1999 tour of properties.* ***Above:*** *Back Fenning Place.* ***Above right:*** *Malcolm Brown, Chairman of the Trust, 1995-2002.*

By 1941 the Trust had converted 60 houses in the west end of Newcastle, and in Gateshead, into homes for over 250 tenants including single people, couples and small families as well as for around a dozen large families of up to nine persons.

Each property had to conform to local authority standards set out in by-laws. Each was provided with a sink, a cold water supply, cooking facilities, a ventilated food cupboard and hanging cupboard. Toilets and coal-houses for each dwelling were provided at the back of the houses, and shared bathrooms in each house were supplied with hot water from a boiler stoked by one of the tenants. Some flats were provided with hot water directly to their own kitchens and bathrooms whilst others were self-contained with their own hot water systems.

St John's Church was also very much involved in the Trust and raised money to buy and refit a number of large houses. The Parish magazine of May 1932 refers to a leaflet "Practical Ways of Helping the Unemployed" and appeals to members of the congregation to invest their money with the Newcastle Housing Improvement Trust suggesting that "25 people saving 2/6 a week could rehouse one family a year".

The war years of 1939-45 inevitably hampered further progress. Housing was generally in short supply with attics and cellars occupied as well as the floors in between. The aim of the Trust however was to continue to help those who stood very little chance of finding a home on the local Authority waiting list for a council house, single people couples and the retired whose need was particularly desperate. The Rent Restrictions Act, intended to prevent exploitation of tenants by landlords, now ironically made it harder for the Trust, whose aim was specifically to provide low rent property, to raise enough money in rental income to buy new property or improve existing stocks. A post war house price boom also meant that property, which before the war could be bought for as little as £150, now cost more than £400.
Although the Trust was unable to buy much new property in the decade following the war's end it did do other excellent work. The management of some 46 privately owned flats had been handed over to the Trust, in addition the Trust was now managing 69 tenancies on behalf of the Church Army Housing Ltd as well as more than 30 tenancies held by other charities.

In 1987, by which time the Trust had become the Newcastle and Whitley Housing Trust Ltd, the organisation had no fewer than 460 tenants in Newcastle, Gateshead and North Tyneside and was opening its first housing development for the elderly in Blyth. Ten years later more than 800 properties were being managed by the Trust which now received a two million pound boost to its finances with a loan from the Royal Bank of Scotland - a very large sum of money compared to the £650 which its first house had cost back in 1929 and which it had converted into five flats.

***Above right:** Steve Ward pictured with the Deputy Head, Julia Bayes and pupils at South Benwell Primary School.* ***Right:** St Anthony's Court, Walker, the Trust's popular sheltered housing scheme.*

and that objective has remained a constant throughout the passing years. More recently, since 1996, the Trust has become a major provider of housing for people with more complex needs such as 'learning difficulties', physical disabilities and dementia. The Trusts' involvement in the Earls House Hospital re-provision for example at the start of the new century would be the largest single contract of that kind ever won by the Trust.

Since 1964 the Trust as a housing association registered with the Housing Coprporation has been able to access government funding to help it in its work of acquiring, building and refurbishing properties.

Over the years the Trust has faced many challenges, particularly meeting the ever increasing demand for its services and securing capital to develop its housing portfolio. Growth had been steady, but piecemeal, in the early days, with a few new properties acquired infrequently each year depending on fund-raising efforts and borrowing. That slow growth has however been sustained over many decades and has inevitably led the once tiny organisation to become a major provider of rented housing in the 21st century.

From the outset the Trust has always aimed to provide housing and practical support to those on greatest need, The Trust likes to see itself as a caring, professional organisation with its tenants at the centre of its aims and objectives. Trust staff and members pride themselves on their relationship with the Trust's tenants and work very hard to involve tenants in shaping the services they are offered through a very active Tenants' Forum which holds meetings every month.

For the future the Trust sees itself as continuing to provide good quality general family and more specialist supported housing. But it will continue to invest in its existing housing stock and meet housing needs wherever it can.

Octavia Hill died in 1912 but the movement she promoted lives on. And surely nowhere is her memory so well honoured than in Newcastle, and in the continuing work of the Newcastle & Whitley Housing Trust.

Top left: *The Plessey Court development.* ***Above left:*** *Chief Executive, Douglas Taylor, signing an historic loan agreement with Ken Kerr of the Royal Bank of Scotland.* ***Right:*** *Douglas Taylor, current Chief Executive.*

Transport

What a busy place Pilgrim Street had become. Even in 1947, the road was crammed with traffic dodging its way in and out of routes used by the trams. Even though petrol rationing was still in force, there were enough car drivers who had been able to eke out their allowances to help create the crowded scene. Possibly, some had a friend in the know who helped them get supplies from the black market. Unfortunately, this was something of a growth industry as those with an eye for the main chance did not mind breaking the rules or breaking the law. Nylon stockings, petrol, luxury goods were to be had, but at a price. Those who were fair minded or too timid to use under the counter methods relied heavily on public transport. The queue of trams along Pilgrim Street would all have been full as they clanked and sparked their way along the tracks that saw their first electrically powered vehicle in December 1901. Within three years most of the city's roads had trams moving along them. This was a credit to the Corporation as the Parliamentary Act permitting the building of an initial 21 miles of track and overhead cabling had only been passed in 1899. Despite the amount of custom that the trams enjoyed, the last one ran in 1950 and passed into the history of transport, much to the regret of those who saw them as part and parcel of city life.

Below: Central Station on 6 February 1952 had gobbled up a meal of travellers and commuters who had abandoned their cars for the comfort and reliability of travel by rail. Who can say that now? In some things, the good old days really were just that. 'Even the children know it', as one advertising poster put it when extolling the virtues of a 14 day return to Whitley Bay where we would be spending our summer holidays. Rail travel was very popular and we were advised to book well ahead, though early February did seem a little extreme. For those wanting to enjoy a day out before then there was always the steeplechasing at Sedgefield for a 6s 3d (31p) return or the cultural delights of York for half a guinea (52.5p). Central Station has been with us a long time. When Robert Stephenson's High Level Bridge, with its twin road and rail decks, opened in 1849 it paved the way for the station. Queen Victoria's arrival for the grand opening was accompanied by a magnificent salute from the castle guns. John Dobson's design was so impressive that it helped his work to be acknowledged as far afield as the Paris exhibition of 1855, where he was awarded a gold medal. Central Station's handsome architectural lines have stood the test of time and are a fine example of Victorian design and craftsmanship.

Right: These single deckers, the SOS IM4 and 538 dating from 1931, followed by the SE6 2 and SE4 Leylands, had no destination flagged up at the front. Just a single word, 'workmen', described the purpose of this transport. The leading bus has some form of camouflage paint on the roof in an effort to help it hide from prying eyes in the skies above. The transport fleet was taking the men off to do essential work for the war effort, but kept the actual destination a secret. The workers could have been heading for the shipyards, engineering works, armament plants or munitions factories but, wherever they were headed, the importance of their input could be guaranteed. Although there is only a handful of women to be seen in these ranks, elsewhere there would have been larger numbers undertaking vital work as they did the jobs left behind by those who had been called up into the armed forces. Some men in reserved occupations felt embarrassed that they could remain at home while others went off to fight, but their skills were being used to the same end, namely the preservation of the nation. The photograph is undated, probably because of censorship restrictions that the government imposed to prevent valuable information leaking to the enemy. 'Be like dad, keep mum,' we were told.

WORKMEN
WORKMEN
RKMEN
NORTHERN

Below: Forget the Millennium Dome: in June 1951 when this scene was captured by the cameraman the thing to see was the Skylon, the major feature of the Festival of Britain seen advertised here on the canopy above the Worswick Street bus station. The sign on the fascia of the enclosed bus station advertises an excursion to travel to London and see the Festival of Britain. Tens of thousands of visitors from the North (and indeed from all over the world) attended the exhibition which was held on the South Bank of the Thames. The line up of buses, most of which date from the 1940s, and featuring the famous 'Shop At Binns' adverts, readily calls up memories of the sights and smells of those sturdy workhorses which clocked up millions of miles during their long years of service. Travel by bus has changed dramatically since this picture was taken: one-man (and it invariably was a man not a woman) operated services were all but unknown and conductors took our pennies when there were still 12 of them to a shilling. And none of that 'No Smoking' nonsense - seat backs even featured metal plates on which you could strike a match in order to light up your Woodbine.

Right: The photographer of this aerial view is to be congratulated in bringing this stunning view to us. Captured in 1950, the shutter clicked to take in the Haymarket, St Thomas' Church, the bus stands and the war memorial. Even now, despite the enclosure of the bus station and the looming presence of the 1968 civic centre behind the church, this is an instantly recognisable part of the city. Looking roughly northeast from above Percy Street, 'Winged Victory', the war memorial, rises in the centre of the image as a 70 feet high tapered, octagonal column that is a tribute to those who fell in the South African campaign or Boer War. It was during that conflict that the phrase 'concentration camp' came into being - a term with even more horrific connotations during World War II. St Thomas' Church, built in 1850, stands somewhat confusingly on St Mary's Place. This address was taken from the former medieval leper hospital, St Mary Magdalene, that once stood near here. In modern times, the road leading left from the memorial goes to Barras Bridge before heading off to a junction with the A167M from where it becomes the Great North Road to Gosforth and beyond.

Burton
VERNONS

Left: Northumberland Street has been the town's most important shopping street since the 1920s, and it remains one of Britain's busiest shopping streets outside of London.It certainly looks busy enough in this chilly lunchtime view captured for posterity in 1959 and which shows Northumberland Street with the junction of Blackett Street and Pilgrim Street. How this scene has changed: take a careful look and note the trolley-bus wires and the complete absence of road markings. Who then would have predicted a world which all too soon would contain speed cameras, breathalysers and parking meters?Back in the days when this photograph was taken Northumberland Street was still the main through route from London to Edinburgh. Today policemen directing traffic have long since been replaced by traffic lights, but here we can still see policemen doing what was then an everyday job for them, trying to untangle traffic jams. Filling the upper left part of the frame is the distinctive old Burton's building which has made way in more recent times for the Monument Mall shopping centre.

Above: The open aspect of the forecourt and the garb of the men at the pumps might make a reader think of Route 66 or some other American highway. Nothing so fancy, for this was the face of Benton Oval service station on 2 August 1962. The various cans were all made to exact specifications of volume and capacity and were being filled by the men from the weights and measures inspectorate. It was their job to check that retailers were not fiddling their customers and, having finished here, were off to check on the optics and pint pots of some poor landlord or the scales used by an unsuspecting grocer unaware of their imminent arrival. Usually the general public is suspicious and aggressive towards certain types of officialdom, but these men were on our side and if they could squeeze an extra drop of fuel from those pumps for our tanks, so much the better. The self service petrol station was becoming more common in the early 1960s. Where once an attendant leapt from his kiosk, checked oil and water levels, wiped the windscreen and then dispensed the petrol for us there was now no one in sight. We were left to do the lot for ourselves in the name of progress.

Sporting life

Below right: Little did we know it, but on 11 September 1938 we were starting the last season of proper league football for another seven years. In less than a year from the date of this 'action shot' those two words would come to mean something chillingly different. A popular trick quiz question is the one that asks, 'Which soccer club held the FA Cup for seven years?' Groans can be heard when the answer 'Portsmouth' is given, followed by the explanation that it was won in 1939 and not surrendered until 1946. Billy Cairns was approaching his 26th birthday and in his prime when photographed leading the Newcastle line. Like so many of his contemporaries, he lost his best playing days to the war. Although short for a centre forward at 5 ft 9 ins, he had a spring-heeled leap, as Burnley's defence could testify. United bought him from Stargate Rovers in 1933 for £25 and gave him a free transfer in 1944 to Gateshead, for whom he netted 42 times in one special season. Billy was never in the same category as Gallacher, Milburn, MacDonald and Shearer, but he knocked in 54 goals in 91 matches for the Magpies. He signed for Grimsby in 1946, become club captain and did not hang up his boots until 1954, by which time he was 42.

Far right: No nostalgic look back at the middle of the last century would be complete without mention of one of the north east's finest sons. John Edward Thompson Milburn, 'wor Jackie', was born in Ashington in 1924 to a family whose lineage would also produce the World Cup winning Charlton brothers. He signed for Newcastle United from his home town club in 1943 and made his debut in 1946 against Millwall. He stayed at St James' Park until 1957, by which time he had become a national legend and household name. That was not easy in the days before television made superstars of the humblest of talents, but Jackie's ability on the field was there for all to see from the terraces. Though under six feet in height he was a powerful man who was also nimble enough to turn on a sixpence and lose a centre half in a flash. In 395 games for United he racked up 199 goals, including the then quickest one scored in the FA Cup Final when he rattled one past Manchester City's Bert Trautmann to set a record that lasted for over 45 years. Jackie's ability was not fully acknowledged by the selectors of the national team and he won a ridiculously paltry 13 England caps. He had spells as a manager and coach after he hung up his boots, but never scaled the same heights as in his playing days.

Above: Hail the conquering heroes! The crowd is packed tight in Grey Street in May 1955 to welcome home the Newcastle United team fresh from their victory over Manchester City at Wembley. Thousands of supporters filled the city to cheer the trophy-winning lads. The team bus is abreast of the premises of Mawson Swan and Morgan Ltd having just passed Lloyds Bank. On the far left of the picture can be seen the huge plinth on which stands Grey's Monument, the 130ft high tribute to Charles Earl Grey. The monument which has graced the spot since 1838 was built to honour the man who had devoted so much energy to the 1832 Reform Act and helped usher in a new era of increased democracy in British politics. Though 1955 may have been a happy year in Newcastle such happiness was not universal: sadly the year would also be remembered for the terrible Le Mans race circuit disaster in which a Mercedes racing car left the track and crashed into the crowd killing no fewer than 70 spectators .

Below: Gosh what a crowd! Newcastle United football fans had enjoyed themselves in London before taking the short trip up to Wembley to watch the 1951 Cup Final. The opposing team on this occasion was Blackpool FC. Football was a real man's game in 1951 - and if you can see a female form in this throng you've better eyesight than we have! And whatever happened to rattles? These were truly the glory days of football: no body searches before being allowed into the stadium, no pitch invasions nor violence on the terraces, and hence no need to ban beer bottles from the grounds The chap on the front row here not only has his beer bottles, he's even brought a glass to drink from and a biscuit box for his sandwiches. In those days fans didn't need to be caged and be made to watch the game through wire mesh fences as if they were wild animals in a zoo. And how clothing fashions have changed: flat caps may have been on their way out, with trilbies and bare heads increasingly popular, but just count those gabardine rain coats - it looks as though every single supporter on the front row has been to the same gents clothing shop!

NEWCASTLE

Here it is, the centre of the universe. Well, at least that is the case if you are a Magpie fan, for nothing else matters. St James' Park is one of those major football grounds that is close to the centre of the city that it serves, unlike many others that are on the outskirts or have relocated to new sites out of town. Even the prawn-sandwich eaters of Manchester United cannot find a ground in their own city, playing in Stretford, near to Salford Quays. Our footballing shrine is within a stone's throw of the heartland and we are proud of it. Of course it has had a major facelift since this 1975 view, but it has retained the same atmosphere that we have come to enjoy through the roller-coaster of a ride that is the lot of the football fan supporting a team through thick and thin. In 1882 Newcastle had two pioneer clubs in East End and West End and the former soon took over St James' Park from the shortlived Newcastle Rangers' club. However, financial troubles beset West End and it was taken over by its main rival in 1892. The following year, the amalgamated United entered the Football League, drawing its inaugural match with Royal Arsenal. The first Division One title came in 1905, but modern supporters are now interested in when the top trophy will be back at St James' Park, having come close to breaking the Manchester United and Arsenal stranglehold in recent years.

Bird's eye view

Looking east along the Tyne, towards Gateshead Quays on the right, as the river begins its graceful turn towards Tyne mouth and the North Sea, you might wonder what has happened to the Swing Bridge. Has somebody made off with it in the dark of night? Fortunately, it is just a trick played by the camera angle. The lowest of the famous bridges, it is almost completely obscured by the 1,400 feet long High Level Bridge that was built by Robert Stephenson. Combining a road, 85 feet above the river, with a railway another 27 feet above, was a novel piece of imaginative engineering typical of 19th century pioneers in this field. How well their work has stood the test of time. Up and down Britain, Telford, Brunel and the Stephenson family left us a heritage that is both rich and practical. The other bridge that can be seen clearly was designed by Mott, Hay and Anderson, with its towers being the work of local architect R Dick Burns. Built by the Middlesbrough firm of Dorman Long, the George V or Tyne Bridge took three years to construct. Begun in the summer of 1935, the King for whom it was named performed the official opening ceremony on 10 October 1928, though the finishing touches had been applied earlier that February.

Newcastle is well renowned for its up to date face in the world of culture, sport and regeneration, but no look at the city would be complete without a glance at some of its engineering heritage. Six great bridges straddle the Tyne, providing a variety of links to Gateshead and beyond. Pictured here are the High Level Bridge, Swing Bridge and Tyne Bridge. The middle one of these, built in 1876 by William Armstrong (1810-1900), is a hydraulically-operated marvel that is located on the site of the Roman Pons Aelius and a former medieval bridge. This position was the lowest crossing point on the river 2,000 years ago. When the Swing Bridge was being built, two Roman altars dedicated to the watery

gods Neptune and Oceanus were among the important antiquities to be unearthed. The other bridges not in the picture lie a little further west, to the left of the scene. The Queen Elizabeth II or Metro, King Edward VII and Redheugh bridges complete the sextet that is a testament to British engineering. The railway station we can see is another reminder of the work of Robert Stephenson. The northeast was in the vanguard of rail transport, with the Newcastle and Carlisle line being the first one to open that ran across the country. The 'diamond crossing' of interlocking track on the approach to Newcastle was once the busiest and largest railway crossing in the world.

The view northwards across the city clearly picks out the sweep of Newgate Street from Bigg Market, bending to the right as it becomes Percy Street. At the top of this 1950 aerial view, readers with a keen eye can identify the war memorial where Northumberland Street meets Percy Street close to the university building, with part of the Royal Victoria Infirmary behind. Parts of this section of the city have changed with the cutting of John Dobson Street, parallel to Northumberland Street, and the building of the shopping malls, but other landmarks remain clearly visible. The gardens of Eldon Square and Grey's monument stand out near to the centre of the photograph. Just below and to the left of the figure of the old prime minister, we can make out Grainger Market. The original dates from 1835 when it was divided into flesh and vegetable markets, but this burned down in 1901 to be replaced by the one we see here. Whilst some shoppers prefer to go to the designer stores and trendier spots to satisfy their needs, the market continues to attract a healthy clientele for those preferring something a little less pretentious. The building is now protected with a Grade I listing and inside there is a wide variety of goods on sale at the numerous stalls, from food to fashion and books to birthday cards.

CO-OPERATIVE

Here we have a dramatic bird's eye view of the part of the city centre that includes Percy Street, Newgate Street, St Andrew's Church and Eldon Square as it all looked in 1950. We can tell from this photograph that Newcastle was fortunate in comparison with some other major cities in that it escaped the main thrust of the wartime blitz, though if you lived in Gosforth you might take exception to that statement. The Luftwaffe did bomb us, but not to the same degree as Coventry, Manchester, London, Glasgow, Southampton and all those other centres that felt the weight of the enemy's explosive tonnage. Most of our historic buildings survived and we were spared the excesses of modern architecture inflicted upon our urban cousins elsewhere in the country. St Andrew's, perhaps our oldest church, was spared, along with Eldon Square, at the bottom left of the picture. In 1950, trees and pleasant architecture flanked this green oasis. Compare it now with the scene we have in the 21st century as the Eldon Square shopping centre dominates the bottom part of this scene. It hovers over the roadway and throws its shadows across the statue of St George, like some sort of Martian war machine from a story by HG Wells.

From 1721, Town Moor was home to the annual county horseracing meeting, before transferring to Gosforth in 1882. But we know this 30-acre part of the massive 1,000-acre site best as the home of the Hoppings, that great festival of fun and frivolity. In this 1950 aerial view we can make out the dozens of tents, marquees and stalls that provided such jollity and entertainment. In those less politically correct times there were sideshows where we could marvel at the bearded lady, England's answer to Tom Thumb and the man with the anvil head. There were strongmen, dressed in leopardskin leotards, bending iron bars- and boxing and wrestling booths where young men could get their noses bloodied in a vain attempt to impress the girls. There were roundabouts for the kiddies, toffee-apples to rot your teeth and exciting times on the Waltzers being chatted up by darkly handsome young men that mum had warned us about. In the austere times of the immediate postwar years it was good to get the opportunity to forget our problems and let our hair down. We came back from the Hoppings tired out but happy, carrying a goldfish in a little plastic bag. As we entered the front door we did not know who was the happier to see us, dad that we were back safely or puss who was eagerly eyeing up our prize from the hoop-la stall.

Ever since the outstanding Lindisfarne burst onto the pop music scene in the early 1970s, no one could look at such a photograph without starting to hum their seminal anthem 'Fog on the Tyne'. Yet, as all Top-twenty anoraks will know, this popular song only became a big hit for the lads in 1990 when Paul Gascoigne lent his unremarkable musical ability to the group. Anyway, as this was 9 June 1950, any fog in the photograph is probably more attributable to heat haze than anything else. Whatever links we can come up with do not matter, for the stunning scene can easily stand on its own merits. Coal barges, tankers, cargo vessels, cross-river steamer ferries and many more were busy plying their trade alongside yards and quays that hummed with activity. Newcastle's river links with the outside world had helped it grow in importance in medieval times as an exporter of locally produced wool. The town's influence on the nation even extended to its language. In the 16th century locally mined coal, destined for the growing London market, surpassed wool as the town's principal export. The capital city's dependence on sea-borne coal from Newcastle gave rise to the sarcastic phrase 'like carrying coals to Newcastle', which conveys the essence of an unnecessary journey.

At work

Below: Road safety has become part of our consciousness and written into a school's curriculum since the second half of the 20th century began. At one time children played street games and rode their bikes on the carriageway without too much danger, but the growth of traffic in the 1930s threatened to become a major problem for them. Accident statistics rose alarmingly and forced the government into action. Driving tests were instituted, Belisha crossings appeared in towns and a Highway Code formulated. After the war, local councils turned their attention to the protection of children who lacked an awareness of the dangers presented by such simple activities as crossing the road or cycling to the shops. Here, at the primary school in Blakelaw on 3 May 1950, youngsters were being given sound advice on a mock up of a roadway. Stop, look and listen were watchwords being drummed into them, as well as instruction in how to signal correctly and use crossings in safety. Too many of our young people lost their lives through ignorance and it was good to see schemes such as cycling proficiency being promoted. In subsequent years we had the Tufty Club, the Green Cross Code and even a permed Kevin Keegan stopping us running out from behind parked cars. Some of it was a little silly, but it did not detract from the importance of the subject - namely our children's welfare.

Right: In 1898 a locally based soap manufacturer produced a yellowish cake of soap that was to transform its fortune. Thomas Hedley was already a successful company, but when it came up with the name 'Fairy' for its new line a rosy future was guaranteed. Had it just been created with something mundane like 'Hedley's Soap Bar' it is unlikely that the product would have become a household name. Even back in Victorian times firms appreciated the importance of branding and 'Fairy' had just the right connotations of lightness, fancy and youth that helped it become a market leader. The quality was good, but that was not necessarily everything. On 14 May 1952 Hedley's had its headquarters in the Phoenix Buildings on Collingwood Street. By then it was part of the Proctor and Gamble empire, having been acquired in 1930. The soap was being promoted as ideal for both clothes and skin, indeed for everything. Although soap had been around for centuries, the caked variety only became common in the early 19th century and was the preserve of the wealthy until mass manufacturing techniques eventually brought the product cost within the reach of ordinary people. In more modern times washing up liquids, such as Fairy Liquid, have become commonplace and the source of some rather twee TV advertising with simpering little girls and mums with wrinkle-free hands.

Top right: The 1944 Education Act gave all youngsters the chance to have full-time schooling and continue their learning through to their teenage years with a better opportunity for the working classes to access higher education. New schools were built in the immediate postwar years, including a primary, or infant and junior school, at Lobley Hill. These tots were enjoying the delights of the reading corner where such stories as 'The little duck who loved the rain', 'The little red hen', 'Busy Timmy' and 'The new baby' awaited

them. On 20 October 1950 children all over the country were brought up on a diet of Beacon readers, Enid Blyton books and look and say or phonetic teaching. Characters in the stories had traditional roles. Mums brought up babies and dads smoked pipes and mended punctures. Biggles flew the skies and fairies lived at the bottom of the garden. Children devoured books with such regularity that the weekly trip to the library was not enough and their appetites for the written word was augmented by comics that told of the daring deeds of Dan Dare or the Silent Three. Little ones were happy to read about Noddy and the naughty golliwog without being turned into racists and had no need of books that suggested that children should have two male parents. It is refreshing to know that in the 21st century Janet and John are making a comeback.

Below: When Albert Edward, Prince of Wales, laid the foundation stone for the Royal Victoria Infirmary on 20 June 1900 he probably anticipated returning as King Edward VII to preside at the official opening ceremony. His mother was in her declining years and, as we now know, he was to accede to the throne the following year. The infirmary was one of the new breed of hospitals that evolved from the work of pioneering spirits and enlightened souls inspired by the example of Florence Nightingale and her ilk. Instead of gloomy and depressing places, often connected with workhouses, bright, clean hospitals were built to meet the needs of the sick. Newcastle RVI was built to cater for 400 inpatients and had its own outpatient department as well. On site accommodation was provided for 100 nurses and the hospital was constructed in eight pavilions with surgical wards on the ground floor, with medical wards above. Patients actually felt that they could enter the establishment with confidence that they would one day leave in good health. This had not always been the case as many 19th century patients felt that the only exit from a hospital led to the graveyard. By 11 October 1950, when this photograph was taken, there had been another medical revolution. In this case it was linked to the administration of the health service and the birth of the NHS in 1948.

Right: At one time you could shout down a pit and out would pop a centre forward or a fast bowler. But, those days have long gone, as have most of the coalfaces at which these men had been beavering away on 24 April 1950. The coal mining industry was once the barometer for workers' pay and conditions. For a hundred years miners were at the forefront of the drive to make the lot of the working man more comfortable. To achieve this end many sacrifices were made that should not be forgotten. Coal provided the basic fuel to drive the industrial revolution that made our country a wealthy land, yet those who went underground received scant reward for the value of their work and the dangers to which they were exposed. In 1910 violence erupted in Northumberland and Durham coalfields as eight hour shifts and round the clock working was introduced, leading to violent riots at Murton colliery. Miners were at the head of the 'not a penny off the pay' campaign of 1926 that led to the General Strike and were among the marchers from Jarrow ten years later. Union confrontation with successive governments in the 1970s and 1980s was based on less sure ground as alternative power sources were developed and they were not helped by the emergence of Arthur Scargill as the NUM leader in 1981. Prime Minister Thatcher made him a prime target in her crusade to crack the unions. Now that our coal industry is a shadow of its former self, let us not forget those who toiled so hard and the thousands who lost their lives in such disasters as at Hulton, Lancashire in 1910 (350 deaths), Gresford, Wrexham in 1934 (262 deaths) and Easington, Durham in 1951 (83 deaths).

Above: This monster was a 60 ton crane with its test load at British Rail Gateshead pictured on 28 February 1950. Notice how the men in front of the locomotive are dwarfed by the sheer size of the beast behind them. The awesome power of this machine and its predecessors is a testament to the skill and ingenuity of the railway engineers who, for over a century, had provided the country with its great age-of-steam. Even today, young children playing at being trains chuff and puff their way through their games, thanks to preservation groups that have kept alive the locomotives of yesteryear and given modern generations the chance to share in the thrill of being carried along a track as gushes of white smoke billow above their heads. Praise be to Thomas the tank engine and all his friends. Because of such enthusiasts we can still appreciate the joy and excitement that must have been felt by our ancestors. How quaint it now seems to realise that they were initially worried that the speed of rail travel in its infancy might have been too much for the human body to endure. Before long, the railways had revolutionised transport and opened up the country for industrialists and travellers alike. The smashing of the 100 mph barrier in the 1930s and the subsequent raising of the speed records in the years immediately prior to the war provoked great national fervour and pride.

Centre: This was the cutting edge of office technology on 14 February 1952. A magnificent Gestetner duplicating machine stood in the corner, ready to churn out umpteen copies of a letter or minutes of a meeting that the typist was producing on a stencil, seated at her lightweight typewriter. From there she could whisk the 'skin' out from the carriage and mount it on the duplicator's drum. Very modern machines were electrically operated, but others had to be hand cranked to turn out the appropriate number of copies. All the while, the poor typist was conscious of the amount of ink staining her fingers and in danger of spoiling her dress. In the meantime, the boss dictated the next task onto the reel to reel tape recorder for her to play back later, using her earpiece and a foot pedal to control the desktop machine. The woman behind him probably doubled as secretary and bookkeeper. She would have been able take dictation at 120 words per minute, having learned Pitman's shorthand at night school or secretarial college. The pecking order in this office was clearly defined. The person in charge just had to be male and he reinforced his authority by facing away from his subordinates. The secretary had a bigger desk than the typist and dressed more primly, as befitted her status. The third in line was rather too jolly in her choice of patterned frock and could not hope to advance until she had drabbed down a little.

Bottom: Oh those days of Latin primers, log tables and PT outside in the freezing cold. Then there were the school dinners eaten at long refectory tables, with our bottoms aching on hard, wooden benches as we tucked into lumpy potatoes, overcooked carrots and gristly meat and looked forward to sago pudding to follow. The happiest days of your life? They were when we look back, but at the time we were hard pressed to think so. Yet there was a strong feeling of camaraderie as we mucked in together at the Royal Grammar School on 15 October 1951. Born in the 1930s, we were sure we would forge a new order, avoiding the pitfalls that took our parents into a world war. History will decide whether or not we succeeded. Those of us on the benches are now drawing our pensions, but we can still recall some of the great mates we made and the scrapes we got into. We are now reliving some of those moments on friendsreunited.com. The first school stood in Westgate at the hospital of St Mary the Virgin. It was demolished in 1844 and, after several temporary homes, moved to Rye Hill in 1870 before settling in the imposing buildings at Eskdale Terrace, Jesmond. Among its famous old boys was the late Brian Redhead, the journalist and broadcaster.

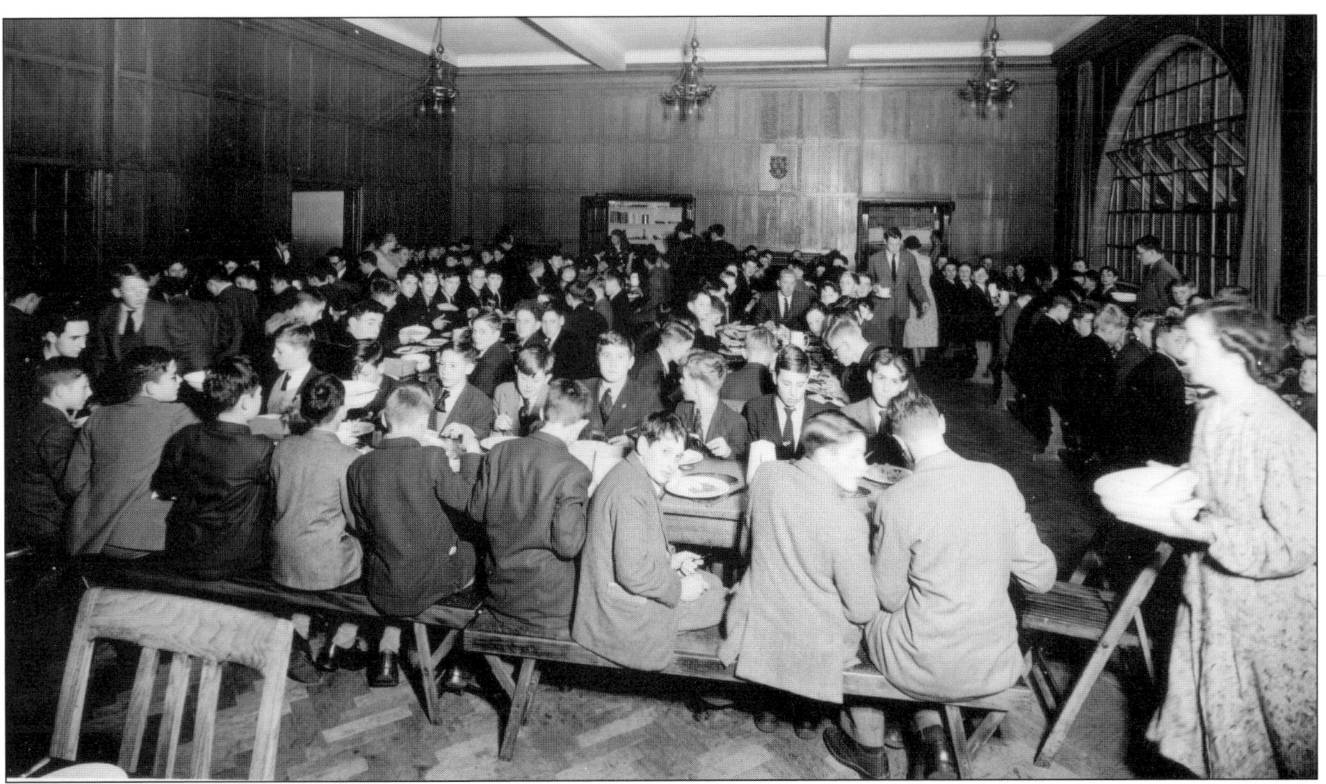

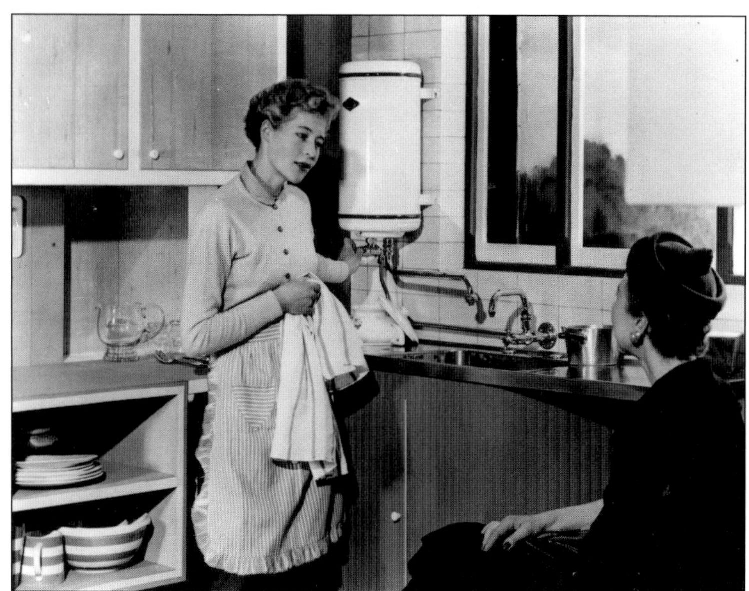

Left: We now take our central heating, with its double radiators and constant supply of hot water, for granted. But that was not the universal situation on 20 December 1957 when the North East Electricity Board was demonstrating the convenience of its electrically powered water heater. Instant hot water was just a turn of a knob away. Note how the sink has just a single cold water tap. Some homes still did not have hot water systems throughout the house and had to rely on boiling water on the stove or a kitchen range. Even more modern houses had to depend upon water heated via a back boiler to a coal fire, and immersion heaters were regarded as something of a luxury. This little wall mounted boiler had an advantage over its gas powered counterpart as it was much safer. The latter appliance, still found in some bathrooms today, was notorious for becoming faulty and giving off poisonous carbon monoxide fumes. Everything featured in the photograph is now a period piece, from the neatly permed hairstyles, mock pearl earrings and tight little hat to the plastic sliding doors under the sink and Formica worktops. The crockery is just right for a 1950s' museum. The blue and white hooped pattern of the plates, bowls and milk jug was repeated in countless homes across the country.

Below left: The fleet of cars, vans and lorries belonged to Wright Anderson, Gateshead-based structural engineers and bridge builders, part of the heavy industrial success story of Tyne and Wear that was still an important force in the middle of the last century. It is interesting to note that on 4 February 1952 one third of the drivers was female. This was probably due to the influence of the second world war when women took over many traditionally male roles. With the menfolk at the front, the call went out for the fairer sex to replace them on the factory floor, operating heavy plant, tilling the land and driving ambulances, buses, tractors and lorries. Not surprisingly, when peace came many women objected to the expectation that they would return to the kitchen sink. They had enjoyed the responsibility and freedom of the workplace and were not happy to relinquish all that they had come to cherish in being accepted as equals in employment. The pay may not have been on the same scale; that was something to be fought for by the next generation, but the status was important and was not going to be easily surrendered. Some firms thought it their duty to lay off women and return their jobs to the men coming back from active service, but others adopted a more liberal policy. Wright Anderson was obviously one of those that decided employment was to be had on merit and not because of some sort of outdated sexist divide.

Below: The woman on the left seems to be sitting on an oil drum, but this is just a photographic illusion created by the angle of the shot. She was actually involved in the bottling process at the Lucozade works on Vicars Lane South, Gosforth. The company took hygiene very seriously and, on 27 October 1950, was well ahead of its time in insisting that the employees wore appropriate clothing and head covering whilst at work. Lucozade, first established in 1927, is now a highly successful soft drinks product. As times change so do people and in order to keep a wide customer-base Lucozade has been constantly changing its image and broadening its appeal to the public. When we were little the fizzy drink was seen as a tonic for young children recovering from illness and this was reinforced in TV adverts of the late 50s when a small boy was shown being nursed by his mother. After a draught of the magical liquid he was soon energetic enough to be banging his drum and rolling around. In more modern times Lucozade has turned its attention to a wider audience, promoting itself as an aid to sports stars and invoking the assistance of the computer generated heroine Lara Croft to sell its wares.

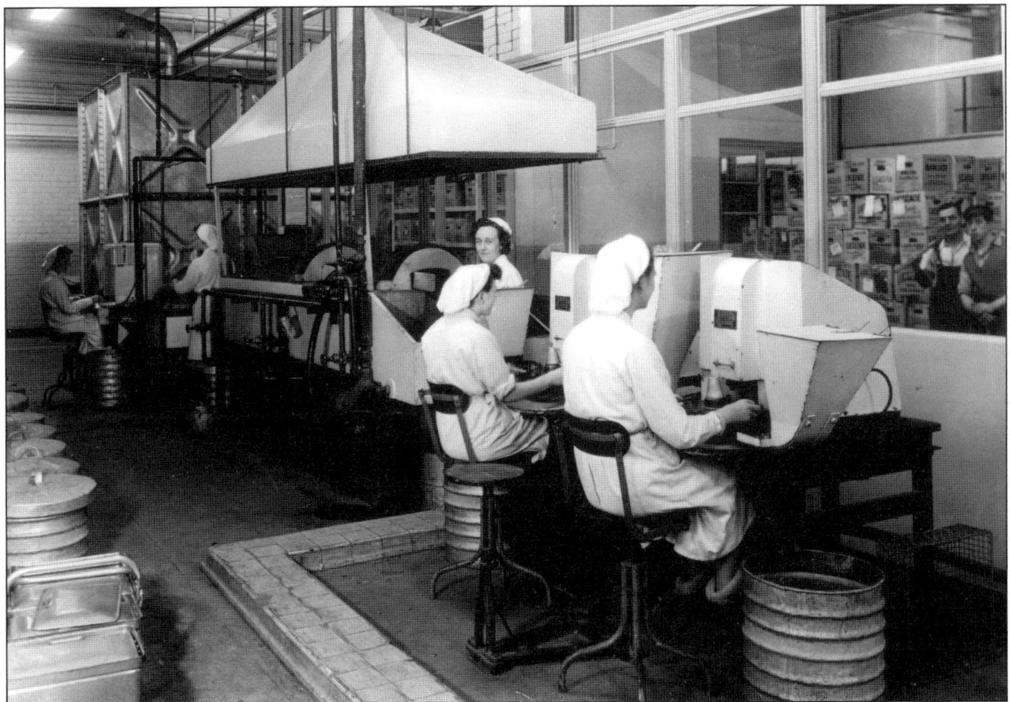

Bottom: Tate's Radio had premises at 95 Grainger Street and 50a New Bridge Street and, as its name suggests, grew up in the age of the wireless when families would gather round their sets in the living room to enjoy the delights of Henry Hall or ITMA coming over the airwaves. In the early 1950s there were great serials like 'Journey into space' and that forerunner of modern soap operas, 'The Archers'. We chuckled at the antics of the Goons and the Clitheroe Kid and even accepted the now crazy idea that Peter Brough, a ventriloquist, should have a radio show with his dummy Archie Andrews. But, as television began to invade our lives, Tate's and its contemporaries had to tool up its workshops to deal with the new phenomenon. It was Queen Elizabeth's coronation that seemed to kickstart a medium that had been struggling to get a foothold in our homes. Many of us watched the ceremony on a friend's flickering black and white set and were immediately hooked. Having bought a TV outright, or perhaps on hire purchase, we got full value for our money, even sitting through a picture of a potter's wheel during an interlude in transmission. Even BBC radio took note, killing off Grace Archer, one of its most popular characters, on the night that ITV was launched in an effort to pinch the limelight.

Right: The men pouring out of Wallsend Shipyard on 15 October 1957, flat caps and all, were enjoying the days of employment before the screw began to turn on the industry that had given them, and their fathers before them, a livelihood upon which they had come to rely. True, things had been difficult during the depression era of the inter-war years, but they had picked up after World War II as Britain replaced its war-ravaged naval stocks. But, once that had been achieved there was a grimmer future in store for these men. Underinvestment and competition from the Far East reduced markets, and shipyards started to feel the pinch. By the late 1970s even the mighty Swan Hunter, also bedevilled by intransigent unions, pulled the plug and others, such as Vickers, felt the pinch. The yards at Wallsend had been an important feature in local life since Victorian times. Companies such as the Marine Steam Company, who built the experimental turbine driven 'Turbinia' in 1897, were flourishing employers. In 1906 Swan, Hunter, Richardson built the 17,000 ton 'Mauretania', Tyneside's largest vessel, but the past counts for little when the bean counters do their sums. However, despite the decline in shipbuilding and repairing, the associated marine and heavy engineering industries remain important to Newcastle. But, like many other former centres of such industries, it now relies heavily upon the service sector for its economic stability.

Top right: From this publicity photograph taken on 13 November 1958, it is not immediately apparent that we are looking at the man who became one of the cornerstone characters of the ITV Sunday night series 'Heartbeat'. Unfortunately, time catches up with all of us as grey hairs abound and waistlines thicken. As that lovable rogue, Claude Greengrass, this actor became a fixture in the programme that charmed millions of viewers with its tales of village life and bobbying in the 1960s. Born Walter Williams on 8 October 1928 in Farnham, Surrey, Bill Maynard had come to the northeast to undertake a promotion for Tyne Tees Television, an ITV company still in its infancy. Typically, two pretty girls had been posed with him in order to

attract more attention. Their skirts were daringly short for the time, showing an amount of knee that got men's hearts all a-flutter. Bill was a comedian and comic actor who had never really hit the big time, but made a steady living in the second division of the variety field. His big breaks were to come in the years to follow when a number of television appearances on comedy shows helped him land the title role in a pilot sitcom, 'Oh No, It's Selwyn Froggitt', in 1974. Two years later this turned into a series that was very popular, thanks to its anarchic humour and the talents of its star. A spin off series, 'Selwyn', followed and led on to Bill being cast as the lead in another top show, 'The Gaffer', in the early 1980s. He also played parts in such diverse movies as 'Confessions of a Window Cleaner' and 'Hear My Song' as well as making his mark on stage in Shakespearean roles that included a notable Falstaff.

Power from the sea

Ships and the sea are never far from the thoughts of Newcastle folk. The Newcastle firm of Stephenson Clarke Shipping Ltd is Britain's oldest shipping company; but though it may have a long history the business is still as important to the nation's economy as when it first began. The company's remarkable story arose out of the relationship between two great cities, London and Newcastle, and the trade between them which made them feel like neighbours, despite being separated by 350 miles of dangerous sea.

Two brothers Ralph and Robert Clarke first bought an interest in a 300 ton sailing vessel in 1730: their limited trading activities were to develop during the following centuries into today's ship-owning and ship-management business.

The sons of a Long Benton vicar the brothers took up seafaring careers, and became master mariners. By buying shares in ships however they gradually established themselves as ship owners, although they still continued to serve at sea themselves for some time. Unhappily, despite a promising start, in Robert's hands the business all but collapsed in the middle of the 18th century, but better times came again.

Happily for posterity Robert Clarke had two sons, John and Ralph. John married Jane Stephenson and moved to London to set up business with his brother Ralph. There they carried on business of ship owners and coal factors; it was in this way that the foundations of the present shipping company were laid.

The core of the company was built on the 'sea-coal' trade from the north east of England to the Thames, providing coal for domestic and industrial use. The coal was often traded by the company as well as simply being transported. John and Ralph also represented their father's and uncle's business in the capital.

In 1792 John Clarke died and his wife Jane took his place in the business; four years after Jane retired Ralph took a new partner, J Burgess.

That was not the last of John and Jane's line however: they had two sons, Robert and Stephenson. Robert, the eldest, had joined the firm in 1806, but when he died at the age of 67 it fell to his younger son, another Stephenson Clarke, who was already in the business, to take over. Stephenson Clarke & Company was formed the following year.

Above: *Robert Clarke, founder of the company.*
Below, both pictures: *Early twentieth century views inside a ship.*

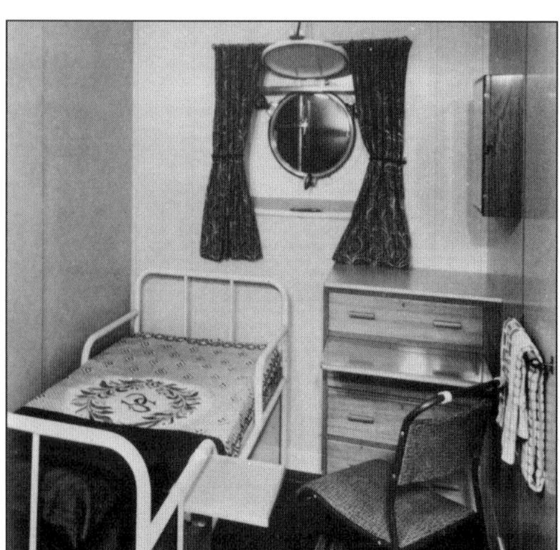

Originally sailing vessels had been used but in 1865 the first recorded steamers 'ME Clarke', 'CS Butler' and 'JM Strachan' were built by Palmers of Jarrow for the company. Five years later Stephenson Clarke had obtained a contract to carry 15,200 tons of coal to Southampton Gasworks in monthly quantities varying between 800 and 2,400 tons. For over a century the company's ships would supply the Southampton Works until carbonation ceased in 1968.

Until 1918 business remained steady, but the years which followed the end of first world war were difficult ones for Stephenson Clarke - nevertheless the period was used to consolidate the business. With the formation of the Normandy Shipping Company in 1915 had come the first working association with the Powell Duffryn Steam Coal Company. That association was strengthened in 1921 by the formation of Maris Export & Trading Company: Powell Duffryn Steam Coal and Stephenson Clarke were the sole partners with a share capital of £250,000.

The Maris Export & Trading Company had been created to manage the export activities of both businesses, dealing in coke, pitch and patent fuels. The Stephenson Clarke fleet was built up by the addition of the 'Vaux', the 'Cranford' and the 'Lys', so that by 1920 7.8 million tons of coal was being delivered by sea.

Colonel Stephenson Clarke retired in 1928 and Sir Stephenson Kent became Chairman. In the world economic crisis which followed however the existing company went into voluntary liquidation, but a new company was soon formed.

For much of the twenties and thirties, though life in the boardroom may have changed, life aboard a steam collier continued exactly as it had been for decades. The journey from Newcastle to London still took around 30 hours, at an average speed of 9 knots. But the vessels had to wait for the tides. Only a couple of ships could make Garrison Point by second tide - but all of them arrived by the third. This fact led to the ships being known as 'three-leggers'. It was extremely hard work battening down the wooden hatches known as 'dominoes', there could be up to 120 of them, and each had to be separately lifted off and stacked away. Later came steel hatch covers, which cut this task from a freezing three quarters of an hour to less than three minutes.

Above: *Father and son, John (top) and Stephenson Clarke.* ***Below:*** *The launch of the Birling,built in 1977 for Stephenson Clarke by Clelands Shipbuilding Company Ltd of Wallsend-on-Tyne.*

Meanwhile some other changes at least made life on board more comfortable for the men. Real bedding was put on board instead of 'Donkeys' Breakfasts', which was the crews' name for the straw mattresses they stuffed themselves.

In the great Depression of the thirties, though it may have been a hard life, at least these men were working when millions of others were unemployed.

By the outbreak of the second world war in 1939 the company had its own fleet of 19 vessels. Only three survived the war intact. 'Borde' was lost to requisitioning by the Admiralty. She was fitted out to become the world's first electromagnetic Mine Destructor Vessel, detonating her first mine on Christmas Eve that first year of the war. During the process Borde's crew had to stand on rubber mats to avoid getting broken ankles from the shock waves.

Broken ankles were not the only danger. Apart from the risk from mines marine hazards included the removal of navigation lights and the need to avoid making smoke. Good firemen stoked little and often so there was less smoke for the enemy to see.

The first Stephenson Clarke vessel to be torpedoed by a fast and lethal German E-boat was 'Broadhurst'. The east coast was particularly prone to this danger, and soon became known as E-boat Alley.

The 111 men whose lives were lost were part of the terrible price paid for our freedom by the seamen of Shields. The area lost more seafaring men in the second world war than any other place in the world.

By the war's end in 1945 the company fleet consisted of just 11 vessels. This number was soon built up by the acquisition of a number of new ships, notably the Seaford 2.

Right: *The Steyning, built by Clelands Shipbuilding Company Ltd in 1983 and still trading within the fleet.* ***Below:*** *Washington - built by Kagoshima Dock & Iron Works Ltd, Kagoshima, carries 8,600 tons of cargo.*

Seaford 2, at 1,500 dead-weight tons, was the first of many purpose-built, diesel-engined colliers. Crew facilities included private cabins, showers and laundries. The increase in the size of the fleet reflected the growth of the power industries.

In early 1950 Stephenson Clarke began to manage hopper barges to dispose of waste at sea. The changing needs of electric power stations led in 1957 to the acquisition of the company's first oil tankers and the renowned 'Flatirons' which were colliers especially built with a low wheel-house to pass under the London bridges in order to be able to deliver coal directly to the upriver power stations.

Undoubtedly however the most innovative development of this period was the result of the gas industry's search for ways of transporting natural gas. Stephenson Clarke bought an American wartime motor ship for this purpose. Re-equipped she became the 'Methane Pioneer' and in 1959 she became the first ship to transport methane.

During the 1960s North Sea Gas began to challenge the coal trade and in 1970 Stephenson Clarke bought some of the vessels previously operated by the Gas Board. Now seemed a good time for a change of company name to reflect its primary role as a shipping company: Stephenson Clarke Shipping Ltd appeared. During the 1970s and 80s the company continued to expand its fleet both in size of ships and in the number owned.

Having become independent in 1992 through a management buy-out the company was now acquired by the International Maritime Group in September 1997. IMG now moved its own headquarters to Newcastle, creating a major maritime corporation in the area and reinforcing the North East's rightful position as an important centre for maritime business.

In the 21st century the Stephenson Clarke fleet of vessel trading throughout Europe carry a diverse range of cargoes. Both the ships and their contents would have been inconceivable to the original Clarke brothers; they would however fully appreciate the dedicated seamanship of the men who still ply their trade upon the waves.

Top: *The Storrington discharging Alumina at Blyth.* ***Right:*** *The Ashington, built in 1979 by Swan Hunter Shipbuilders Ltd, Wallsend & Neptune yards, Tyne.*

Pages of history

When Newcastle's new Central Library was opened to the public in October 1968 the modern concrete building, housing some 150,000 books and public records, was rightly heralded as a great leap forward for the City. But the new library was only the latest manifestation of a cultural progress which had its origins more than a century earlier.

The building of a city library had been mooted as early as 1854, but nothing was achieved. A similar motion was put forward at a Council meeting in 1872 by Henry Newton, and passed by a majority, though disappointingly the Mayor refused to sign the necessary council minutes on a technicality.

Not until 1874 would a Public Libraries Committee be formed, with Councillor Newton as its chairman - a position he would hold until his death in 1914.

For five years there was a running argument about a site. Because the final choice in New Bridge Street, next to the Mechanics Institute, necessitated the demolition of the ancient Carliol Tower, a public enquiry was held by the Lords of the Treasury in 1879 - an enquiry which finally quelled the opposition.

In September 1880 a temporary lending library was opened occupying the ground floor of the Mechanics Institute which was taken over by the new institution. The initial stock was 20,069 books, 2,000 of which came from the MI. With only 972 children's books however the age limit of members was initially restricted to those aged 14 and over.

Astonishingly the books were arranged not by author, or subject, but by size, making it necessary to consult a catalogue to find the volume one might be looking for.

In September 1882 the central library building was finally opened.

Little could those who attended the opening ceremony have predicted that 86 years later there would be another opening ceremony when former Minister of Education Sir Edward Boyle would formally open a second brand new Central Library.

But in whatever building it has been housed Newcastle's Central Library has always been a treasure house of education and entertainment for generations of Newcastle folk - and provided a magnificent memorial to Henry Newton's persistence.

***Above:** Newcastle's old Central Library. **Below, both pictures:** The new Central Library, opened in 1968.*

Getting it together

The Co-op is one of the best known retailing names in Britain. There are some 150 individual Co-operative Societies in the North Eastern and Cumbrian Co-op's 'family tree' which trace their origins to the 19th century.

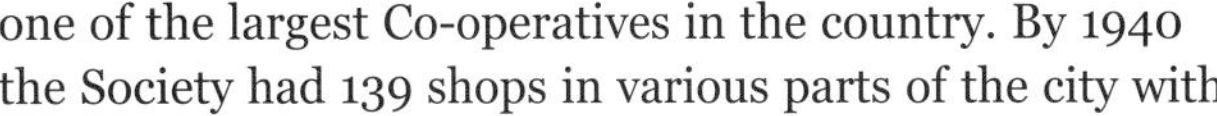

Upperby near Carlisle had a small society as long ago as 1829 whilst in the North East the 'Teesdale Workmen's Corn Association' was established in 1842; the first fully fledged retail society came into being at Blaydon in 1858.

The modern Co-op movement however traces its founding to the Rochdale Equitable Pioneers Society formed in 1844 and whose 28 members pooled their resources to open a small shop from where they sold wholesome food at reasonable prices. By the end of the 19th century there were over 1,400 Co-operative Societies throughout the country.

The Newcastle Society was founded in 1860 and was at first run from a rented room at 18 Nelson Street before growing into one of the largest Co-operatives in the country. By 1940 the Society had 139 shops in various parts of the city with central premises in Newgate Street, a building eventually listed and recognised as one of the finest examples of art deco inter-war architecture in the North.

Owned by its members, money raised by the Co-op was used to invest in the welfare of employees, members and their communities - and the remaining profits were shared out via the famous Co-op dividend or 'divi'.

In 1970 the 31 leading Co-operative Societies in the North East merged to form a regionwide group 'the North Eastern Co-operative Society' whilst on the other side of the Pennines a similar merger soon took place when the Cumbrian Co-operative Society was established by the five major Co-operative businesses between Carlisle and Barrow.

In 1990 the North Eastern Co-op joined forces with the nationally based Co-operative Group (CWS) which the Cumbrian Co-op joined in 1992. Both areas are now united under a Regional Board and Committee structure which operates under the auspices of the Co-operative Group's Central Board. But though some things change other's remain eternal: the Co-op's commitment to values and principles which include honesty, openness and caring for others.

Above: *The Scotswood Road store.* ***Above left:*** *Newcastle's Buckingham Street branch.* ***Left:*** *The Gateshead Society's headquarters in Jackson Street, decorated for the Coronation of King George VI in 1937.* ***Below:*** *Newgate Street store, Newcastle.*

Pork of the town

Back in 2001 there was no question of having caviar or smoked salmon sent in for Roxy Music singing Star Brian Ferry when he was performing at the Gateshead Arena. Instead the veteran singer was actually to be found enjoying the delights of a local pork sandwich, just one of the wide variety of traditional foods made and sold by Dickson's, the well known Pork Butchery chain.

Brian, in fact, bought no fewer than ten pork sandwiches from Dickson's Byker branch so he could share their distinctive taste with other members of his group. 'As soon as he came into the shop I recognised him' said an excited Roxy Music fan Branch Manager, Paul Brown. 'He told me that Tyneside pork sandwiches used to be a favourite of his, and it just goes to show how we Geordies never forget our roots'.

But happily you don't have to be an international pop star to sample one of Dickson's pork sandwiches - anyone can buy them!

Dickson's meat and delicatessen products are available throughout Tyne and Wear and beyond. There can be few local readers who have not at one time or another, had the pleasure of enjoying a Dickson's pie, pork sandwich or perhaps the famous saveloy!

For two generations now Dickson's chain of shops has been satisfying the demanding standards of hungry northerners, and it's still run by the family who started out in business in a fairly small way at the 'Nook' in South Shields back in the early 1950s.

What has since become Tyne and Wear's if not the North East of England's leading meat products company, was founded in 1953 by Irwin and Helen Dickson with help from Helen's sister, Rose and Irwin's brother Tom.

The family connection with the business has earlier roots however, for while both husband and wife had been working separately in the trade from leaving school - in Helen's family, the tradition can be traced back a generation further.

At the turn of the century Helen's father, Fritz Kuch, had left the family farm in the Wurtemberg region of Southern Germany to make a new life for himself in Tyneside.

***Above:** Irwin Dickson and his wife Helen, founder's of the firm. **Below left:** Bobby Thompson, the 'Little Waster' opens Dickson's Wallsend branch in April 1978. **Below:** The crowded Wallsend branch on it's first day of opening.*

as Cook's - the English equivalent of the family name and Fritz worked there until his retirement in the early 1950s.

During this time Irwin Dickson was learning his trade with the Wallsend Pork Butcher, Edward Hay. He had hoped to take over the business on Mr Hay's retirement but again European conflict played an important role in the family's life with the outbreak of the Second World Way disrupting these plans when Irwin was called to serve in the Royal Artillery.

Helen in the meantime, had left home and the family shop to help in another German family's business in Howdon near Wallsend, that of Dorsch on Tynemouth Road.

He worked for Mr Kaufmann at Kays the Pork Butcher's in Newcastle alongside Rosa Kress, a girl from his home region. They married and in I908 Helen was born in Raby Street Byker.

At the outbreak of the First World War, Fritz was interned on the Isle of Man while his wife and, by now, three children were sent back to Germariy. Tragically months after arriving back at the family farm Rosa died at the early age of 32 - leaving the children to be brought up by their grandparents.

The 1920s saw a return to normality so Fritz, his second wife Carolina (Rosa's half sister) and the children returned to England where he opened a shop in Spennymoor. The family later moved to Sunderland, opened a shop in Walworth Street, trading

When Irwin was demobbed he was keen to get back to his trade and with his friend and business partner John Whitfield, took over Dorsch's shop. Another 'partnership' quickly developed as Irwin and Helen were soon married.

Whitfield and Dickson prospered also, John and Irwin working night and day but with meat rationing in force it was never going to be easy.

The shop was out of stock and closed by lunch time most days, but the enterprising pair opened a fish and chip bar in the evenings on Wallsend High Street to fill their time and bridge the income gap!

This page: *The company's Fowler Street premises with the 'new' Sandwich Bar in the late 1970s, above staff wait for more customers and right a view inside the 'cellar' boning area.*

In the early 50s Irwin and Helen now with two small children decided to strike out on their own and moved to South Shields in 1953 the year of Queen Elizibeth II Coronation taking over what had been Newton's on Prince Edward Road in the town.

The next few years found the business growing from strength to strength and in 1959 they followed up that first business venture by taking over the large Town Centre premises of Bernard Tonneson, in Fowler Street South Shields.

The risk paid off and the small family concern soon found itself with a staff of 40 and a much larger customer base.

Success turned to heartache when Irwin sadly died in 1966 at the age of 53.

Helen continued to run the Company aided by her daughter Christine who demonstrated a competence and maturity beyond her 16 years, while son Michael pitched in three years later when he left school.

***Top left and right:** More late 1970s pictures of the busy bakehouse over the shop (left) and preparing sausages for the smokehouse. **Below left and right:** Interior and exterior views of Dickson's Laygate branch in the 1970s.*

The business inevitably faltered to a degree in the difficult years that followed Irwin's untimely death. But by 1975 the new generation had begun to move forward with the acquisition of Albert Dietz's business on Ocean Road. A Sandwich Bar was opened adjacent to the Fowler Street premises in 1976 and thereafter followed year on year growth during which time more shops were opened and several well known local pork butcher's businesses were acquired and given the Dickson's makeover

Apart from that first takeover of Dietz's in 1976, they were Lang's of Wallsend, Mark Faldon in Felling, Hilkert's of Morpeth, John Ternent Guidepost, Maddison's of Blyth , Stuart Day in South Shields, and two sites from Ibbitson's of Sunderland.

Over the years growth saw the need for more space and greater capacity and in 1981 all production had been moved from the Shop/Factory in Fowler Street to a new unit on Rekendyke Industrial Estate. This itself was to

The local Fish Shop owner would peel the spuds for the Pork Butcher's down the road but the Dickson children could be left with the job of finishing them off by taking out the eyes - naturally with help! All those potatoes and onions were destined for the pasties and other savoury delicacies which would one day make the family company a byword for good food across the North East of England.

Dickson's pork sandwiches may be legendary but many exiled Geordies will go misty eyed reminiscing over memories of savouring a Dickson's saveloy dip on a biting cold day.

be outgrown, and in 1992 a purpose-built facility was opened on Middle-fields Industrial Estate in South Shields both to give the Company further room to grow and to keep abreast of today's demanding hygiene and food safety requirements.

The Company's retail activities and current 18 shops cover much of the Tyne and Wear conurbation and Northumberland. Wholesaling activity is spread over a broader area still with deliveries as far north as the Border and south into Yorkshire.

Today the firm is still run by two of the founders three children Michael and Christine Dickson - younger sister Dorothy having moved to France on marrying.

According to Michael and Christine where other children may have played with toy cars and dolls they harboured desires to be a part of the family business. Their parents, to keep them quiet and out of mischief, would sit them on a 'crackit' and give them a stone of onions to peel or maybe a bucket of potatoes to 'eye'.

Top and above left: *Dickson's distinctive shop style begins to emerge in the 1980s.* ***Right:*** *An overview of Dickson's first factory, 1981.*

These days up to 50 tons of product - bakery goods, sausage and delicatessen products and cooked meats leave Dickson's factory each week; a mouthwatering avalanche of food destined for their own shop chain and distribution up to 100 miles beyond to wholesale customers.

In the stands at football clubs it could be Dickson's pies that warm chilled fans on freezing afternoons as well as filling the shelves of many of the region's premier delicatessens and supermarkets. Dickson's really hit the headlines in 1997, a year during which Newcastle United weren't just relying on the likes of Peter Beardsley and Les Ferdinand to bring home the trophies. This time it was the club's pie chefs who were the focus of attention. The Toon Army minced beef and onion pies had been nominated as one of the five best served at football stadia across the country in a competition run by a national football magazine. Loyal football fans could tune in to the Radio 5

Breakfast Show to help a panel of judges composed of the presenters and Total Football Magazine's Editor, Richard Jones, putting their taste buds to the test. Competition and rivalry was fierce as with many aspects of 'The Beautiflul Game' and although the result for Newcastle (and Dickson's) was that of runner up, that was a season when the pies did better than the team!

Meanwhile these days the Dickson team fields far more than a mere 11 players. Although the firm started out with just four people, today Dickson's employs some 260 in shops throughout the region as well as at the 'state of the art' factory in South Shields.

The Dickson family give fulsome praise, not only to the management team they've assembled over the years, but their workforce in general.

'We couldn't have maintained our high standards and continued to grow without a motivated and highly experienced staff. There have been several romances and marriages over the years and many instances of the second generation coming through into the workforce giving the business a family feel at more than one level'. says Michael Dickson proudly.

South Shields M.P. and Education Minister David Milliband praised the contribution the business has made to the local economy at a recent visit to the plant and sent a letter of congratulations from The Houses of Parliament to mark the company's Golden Jubilee year in 2003.

The first shop which Irwin and Helen opened at Prince Edward Road in 1953 is still open and trading strongly, very much part of the fabric of local life where 'Sand Dancers' - regional slang for the folk of South Shields rightly known for their fine sandy beaches - pop in to buy home cured ham and pease pudding from those very same premises though unrecognisable from 50 years ago as it has been enlarged and refitted extensively over the years.

Michael and Christine, Managing Director and Retail Director respcctively, still have a soft spot for the shop and its surrounding area of the Nook. They cherish early childhood memories of the flat above which was their first home as small children, and a still developing shopping centre where everyone knew them and they were safe to roam.

When they were children everything their parents sold from the shop was made on the premises just behind the scenes in the bustling Bakehouse and a 'Back Shop where sausages, hams and their accompaniments were carefully created.

Many of the products are not greatly different from what is sold today although, back then, customers would bring their own basins to the shop to be filled with 'molten' pease pudding to enjoy at home possibly with those famous smokey saveloys - a tradition missed by the older generation.

Top left: *John Savident, Coronation Street's Fred Elliot, tucks into a saveloy sandwich in Jarrow.* ***Above right:*** *Stuart Woods - Branch Manager Houghton Le Spring presents Audrey Harrison with flowers and vouchers to mark her many years of local custom after branch refurbishment.* ***Right:*** *An interior view of the current Fowler Street store.*

Tastes have changed over the years however, and some products once sold in quantity such as pig trotters, pigs cheek and tripe have long gone from the displays whilst other traditional foods such as black or white pudding have enjoyed something of a revival and appear on many a sophisticated restaurant menu these days. Breads and an ever broader range of savoury pastry products - all now baked instore - freshly cut cooked meats, coleslaws, Dickson's sausages, bacon and a tempting sandwich bar compete for the attention of today's shoppers.

One item which remains practically unique to the Dickson empire is that beech-smoked saveloy: served hot in one of their fresh baps with pease pudding, sage and onion stuffng and a judicious dollop of English Mustard, it remains a gastronomic delight throughout the Tyne and Wear conurbation - although Michael admits that their branches further north up in Northumberland remain cautious converts!

He feels confident that the 21st Century may see a taste for this delicacy spreading further afield.

Coronation Street's Fred Elliot may be the undisputed sausage king in fictional Weatherfield and the best known butcher in the country, but when it came to the real thing he was the first to take his hat off to Tyneside's leading Pork Butchers. During a visit to Jarrow's Viking Shopping Precinct in 2001 'Fred - famous actor John Savident - called into Dickson's busy local branch arid tried this Geordle fayre himself. And his verdict? He quipped 'I've heard that a saveloy dip is very popular in these parts but I'd never had one before. Very tasty , I'll have to tell our Ashley about it and maybe we'll be selling them down't Weatherfield way shortly'.

One thing is for sure, if the Coronation Street cast were to start eating saveloys on national television they could well become a new national dish rather than being restricted to the North East - but maybe we prefer it that way up here as it's part of our distinct local identity. One thing is for sure, if saveloys do take off there's no doubt that Dickson's will be in prime position to satisiy that demand

With more shops in the pipeline and a multi-million pound expansion programmne pending at the Company's food production facility, the future certainly looks bright for Dickson's.

The Company has certainly come a long way in the years since 1953 when Irwin and Helen put all their savings in that very first shop in South Shields. A lot of hard work and determination has not only made the Dickson name one which is instantly recognisable across the region, but succeeded in creating a brand name which today is synonymous with a wide range of traditional quality meat products.

Top left: *The company's Retail Management Team with Intermediate Food Hygene Qualifications, 2000.* ***Top right:*** *Easter 2002, Michael Dickson and Rt. Hon. David Milliband M.P. review factory expansion plans.* ***Left:*** *Les Ferdinand and Dickson's 'Toon Army Pie'.* ***Below:*** *Christine and Michael Dickson at Prince Edward Road - 50 years on!*

Generations of power

In 2003, after 76 years, Northern Electric said goodbye to its historic headquarters in Newcastle's Carliol House and moved to a new building in Grey Street. But despite its new building Northern Electric's commitment to its historic roots in Newcastle remains as strong as ever.

NESCo, the original private company which would become Northern Electric, was a pioneer, nationally and internationally, in both power generation and supply. The electricity industry was nationalised in 1948, and in this region the North Eastern Electricity Board (NEEB) replaced NESCo and a number of smaller private and municipal supply organisations. In 1989 however, as part of the privatisation of the industry, NEEB became Northern Electric and in the following year was floated on the stock exchange as a public company.

In late 1996 Northern Electric became part of the world energy group CalEnergy - now MEHC - based in the USA and a new era began. But what of Northern Electric's origins?

The North East of England has always been at the forefront of developments in electricity - Joseph Swan invented the electric light bulb and gave its first public demonstration to the Newcastle Chemical Society in 1878. Lord Armstrong installed Swan's lights in Cragside Hall powered by the first domestic hydro-electric generator in 1880. And Charles Parsons subsequently invented the first steam turbine in Newcastle, where it was soon used to generate electricity.

The Newcastle upon Tyne Electric Supply Company (NESCo) was incorporated in 1889 with a capital of £12,000, and by 1890 was supplying electricity from its Pandon Dene power station on the east side of the city.

Above centre: *Joseph Swan's incandescent lamp, first demonstrated to the Newcastle Chemical Society in 1878.* ***Right:*** *Pandon Dene Generating Station which began supplying electricity for NESCo in 1890.*

Newcastle in fact had two supply companies with the Newcastle upon Tyne and District Electric Lighting Company (DISCo) also being formed in 1889. DISCo was owned by Charles Parsons whose steam turbine generators were installed at Forth Banks by the river.

The generating station at Pandon Dene initially consisted of two small 75 kilowatt generators. Further generators were later installed, the largest of which was 500kW. At the power station coal was delivered by horse and cart: the coal then cost just three shillings and sixpence (17.5p) per ton.

Charles Merz and others at NESCo saw that there was little future in small-scale localised operations. They also saw the potential for capturing the growing shipbuilding and engineering industry of Tyneside for electricity and so the use of electricity for general power purposes began to be actively promoted.

Merz was also consulting engineer to the Walker and Wallsend Company: in 1899 he planned a power station at Neptune Bank Wallsend with William McLellan and RP Sloan. Neptune Bank was acquired by NESCo in 1901.

NESCo now became the first electricity generator in the country to supply three-phase electricity operating at a pressure of 5,500 volts. Westinghouse had established three-phase AC distribution in the USA - a form of power

best suited to industrial applications, whilst lower voltages could be supplied to domestic customers.

Neptune Bank was much celebrated in its day. It was regarded not just as the fount of electric power supply in Tyneside but also as 'the beginning of the era of electric power utilisation all over the kingdom' as The Electrician journal later put it, lauding NESCo as the first statutory undertaking in the United Kingdom to supply electric power in bulk for motive power to industry.

Neptune Bank originally contained four 700kW alternators; these were later augmented by two 1500kW alternators driven by steam turbines made by Parsons; they were the largest of their kind in the world at the time, and operated so successfully that Cunard was persuaded to go for propulsion machinery of the same type for The Mauritania.

Neptune Bank would lead the world in power station development for the next 30 years.

A new power station opened at Carville in 1904 which supplied both collieries and the North Eastern Railway for the electrification of the track between Newcastle and Tynemouth. It also supplied power via the High Level Bridge to Gateshead and to the north east of County Durham via a cable tunnel from Carville to Hebburn a tunnel constructed at a depth of 120 feet which was 1,000 feet long and six feet in diameter.

Top: *The Travelling Showroom arrives at an outlying electrified village in the 1920s.* ***Above:*** *W Farrel on duty at Dunston 'A' Power Station in 1931.* ***Right:*** *A Jointers' team, from left to right R Short (Jointer), T Redhead (Jointer's Mate), R Stage (Jointer's Mate).*

Carville was a landmark in power station design and secured the reputation of the Newcastle based consultants and designers Merz and McLellan. It was the largest public supply station in Europe, and the first of any size to be powered by Parsons' steam turbines ten times the average size then being installed across Britain.

In 1906 NESCo became the first undertaking to adopt balanced electrical protection gear of the Merz-Price system which significantly improved reliability. That gear would form the basis of almost every other form of automatic electrical protection.

In that same year NESCo also became the first to use 'metal-clad' switchgear in its substations, a decision which would bring to Tyneside the important switchgear industry of which Reyrolle and Company would become central. In 1906 NESCo installed the first such switchgear at the Swan Hunter yard.

NESCo had extended its operations by building a transmission system of underground cables and overhead power lines, at first using 6kV before the company became, in 1906, the first to introduce 20kV transmission, an improvement which minimised power losses over long distances.

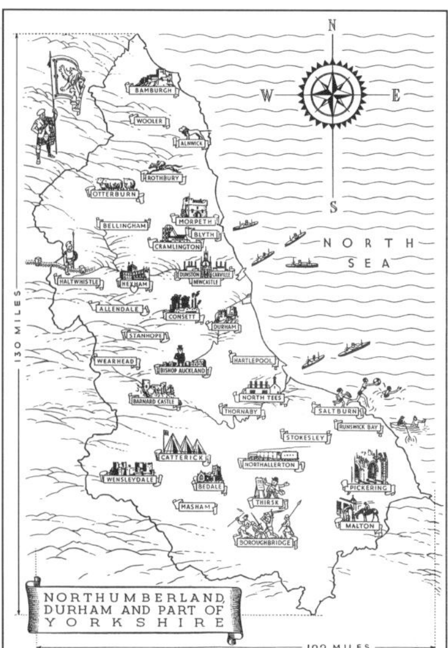

Meanwhile DISCo remained a separate lighting enterprise, whilst at the same time several local authorities in the region operated their own municipal lighting stations which also sold power to industry.

The Newcastle Corporation used its own power station at Manors to power the tramways; Middlesbrough and Tynemouth however took their supplies from companies in the NESCo group for distribution on their own networks.

In 1889 NESCo had supplied electricity for lighting within an area of just 11 square miles; by 1914 the system covered 1,400 square miles. By then the conversion to three-phase 40 Hz AC was well under way and was to be the key to large scale interconnected operation, the largest integrated power system in Europe at the time, and making possible the creation of large central generators with small reserve plant.

Top left: *A linesman perched high above Newcastle.* ***Above:*** *A 2000 volt/220 volt kiosk type substation.* ***Below left:*** *A map of the area in which the Company was authorised to supply electricity.* ***Below:*** *The control room in the 1950s.*

After the first world war ended in 1918 demand rose steeply, and in 1924 NESCo was the first electricity authority in the country to adopt 66,000 volts (66kV) for transmission purposes. High voltage lines were run between the Tees and the Tyne and north to Bedlington in the Northumberland coalfield. In built up areas the company became the first to make commercial use of underground cable operating at 66kV.

Such efficiency and economies of scale benefited everyone. In 1899 the cost of electricity had been four pence; by 1905 the cost was just a fraction over one penny per unit. In the first decade of the 20th century sales increased by a factor of 30, far in excess of growth elsewhere; the load factor now averaged 45 per cent compared to little more than 20 per cent in other industrial areas of the country.

When the Government set the scene for establishing the national grid it was NESCo which provided the model for that grid.

Even during the depression of the 1920s demand for electricity continued to grow, Carliol House, completed between 1924 and 1927, was built as NESCo's new headquarters and would remain as the headquarters of Northern Electric until 2003. Carliol House was Newcastle's first important modern office building in the modernised classical style of the inter-war period. The building incorporated many technical innovations that made it architecturally important. It is made of reinforced steel, a method imported from the USA by the building's

Meanwhile another local first was the principle of centralised control: displaying, controlling and operating the high voltage network from a central control room.

The first system control room was in Carville. The control diagram took up 960 square feet and displayed the generating stations, substations and transmission and distribution network; it was run with the help of the company's own private telephone system.

Top left: *Carliol House, Company head office until 2003.* ***Top right:*** *An electricity sub-station.* ***Above left:*** *One of the company's many showrooms.* ***Right:*** *An electricity showroom at Carliol House in the 1930s.*

architect L Couves of Newcastle. An innovative heating system used 60 tons of electrically heated water circulating through coiled pipes in the ceilings, whilst it was one of the first buildings in the world to incorporate an integral vacuum cleaning system in which cleaners were plugged straight into the walls.

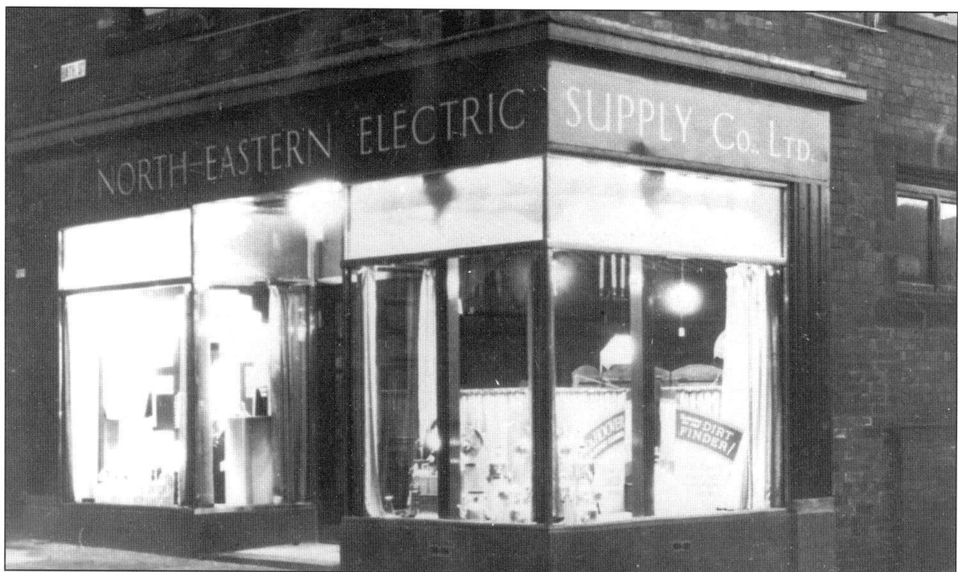

The high-speed electric lifts too were considered to be the most up to date in the country travelling at 430 feet per minute - the fastest in Britain, and possibly in the world at the time.

The building also incorporated a luxury cinema and lecture theatre with seating for 70, used to educate consumers by means of lectures and demonstrations.

The uniqueness of the building was further underlined by the fact that it was faced with Portland stone rather than Newcastle's traditional sandstone. The grandeur of the interior was continued inside with the wide use of marble and mahogany. The mixture of Art Deco and stripped classicism with a distinct Egyptian flavour was a popular feature of many commercial buildings of this period.

Meanwhile the use of electricity in the home was beginning to make life easier and more enjoyable for everyone, not least housewives: after electric lights had come irons, heaters, and fans followed by cookers, washing machines and fridges.

The growth in the use of electrical appliances in the home was actively promoted by NESCo through its shops and mobile showrooms. As a result, throughout the 1930s and beyond, the number of connected customers in the city and the amount of electricity they used grew dramatically.

Use of electricity in the countryside was boosted in 1934 when the Royal Agricultural Society's show was held in Newcastle. Lower electricity distribution costs heralded a drive towards rural electrification which after a pause from 1939-45 resumed after the second world war and would eventually be completed in the 1950s and 60s.

The post-war drive to expand the electrical network was extremely successful. By 1952 around 80 per cent of rural premises were receiving supplies though the balance of farms and other rural communities had to wait for up to ten years more to be connected.

Top right: *A North-Eastern Electric showroom in the 1950s.* ***Above:*** *An evening view of Northumberland Street in the 1950s.* ***Left:*** *Electricity pylons being erected in 1983.*

At the same time NEEB was concerned to standardise distribution voltages which varied throughout the area and to standardise prices so that all its domestic customers paid the same rates.

A great expansion of the network after the second world war ended in 1945 increased the number of staff working for the newly created NEEB to a peak of 9,000 in 1965 (increasing efficiency would see that number fall to 3,500 by the end of the century).

Immediately after the war the NEEB's largest customer was the coal industry which took as much electricity as all the other domestic and commercial customers put together. Today, with the coal industry all but gone, demand is much more evenly distributed between domestic customers and industry.

Throughout the 1950s and 60s price increases to customers were below the rate of inflation, despite the cost of developing the network, and there was a significant growth in off-peak electricity available more cheaply at night. All this changed however from the early 1970s when the twin shocks of miners' strikes and the Middle East Oil Crisis made electricity more expensive to produce and distribute: prices rose accordingly.

Suddenly energy conservation was on the agenda and the days of 10 per cent annual growth were at an end.

Happily for everyone prices would however fall again, quite dramatically in some cases, and customers of Northern Electric have subsequently seen smaller bills, better service and rising investment in a company which pays a strong and positive role in the local community.

Northern Electric was bought in 1996 by CalEnergy, an American company since renamed MidAmerican Energy Holdings Company or MEHC. Two years later the company began selling both electricity and gas; it was the first company to offer such a dual package.

In 2000 MEHC was acquired by a group led by Berkshire Hathaway, the investment vehicle of Warren Buffet one of the wealthiest men in the USA. More change soon followed. Northern Electric now sold its power supply business to Innogy in return for the electricity distribution business of Yorkshire Electricity. Northern Electric's main focus would now be on delivering electricity throughout almost 100,000 km of cable to over 3.6 million customers. That fine focus would be increased in 2002 when Northern Electric's retail appliance business was sold to its managers.

Though in the reign of Queen Victoria the future of the electricity industry may have been unpredictable, one thing we can say with certainty today is that one way or another Northern Electric is here to stay.

Top left: *The board visiting a meter station in 1985.* ***Left:*** *The extent of Northern Electric's area since it combined with Yorkshire Electricity.* ***Below:*** *Technicians still have to climb great heights to carry out maintenance of modern electricity pylons.*

A case history

From the Shell Scandal of 1915, right through to the second world war, and on to more recent conflicts, a plant at Birtley has produced large calibre empty ammunition for Britain's armed forces. That plant, originally known as the National Projectile Factory, is now officially titled BAE SYSTEMS, RO Defence, Birtley, though it is still known throughout the area as the 'ROF' - the Royal Ordnance Factory, an institution directly descended from an organisation founded by Henry VIII in the 16th century.

Two centuries ago the Emperor Napoleon famously remarked that an army marches on its stomach. What he meant was that an army which does not have enough food to sustain it during a campaign is worse than useless. In the 1860s the American Civil War demonstrated a new military axiom: that the side with the greatest industrial output behind it will win the war.

In the summer of 1914 the German Armies of Kaiser Bill, invaded France by way of neutral Belgium. Britain's treaties with both countries obliged her to wade in against the aggressor. War was declared on 4th August, and what the Kaiser reportedly described as a 'contemptible little army' was sent across the Channel to face the Germans: in the other direction came a flood of Belgian refugees.

Right: *Building works at Birtley, 1916.* ***Below:*** *Belgian workers and wounded Belgian soldiers, 1917.*

Britons of all ranks and classes were outraged at the German invasion and flocked to recruiting stations by the hundred thousand. Many were desperate to get to the front before the war ended and revenge the atrocities committed by the Germans in Belgium: bayoneting babies, violating nuns and using living priests as clappers in cathedral bells. Such 'atrocities' were mostly lies, but they were widely believed and fuelled an extraordinary enthusiasm for war.

And even if the stories about the Germans were not true it was time that Johnny Hun, who had been getting too big for his boots, was given a bloody nose. The only worry most young men had was getting to the front in time to join in: after all the war would probably be over by Christmas, wouldn't it?

Some hope. The war dragged on for four hellish years. The stalemate of trench warfare was soon established as both sides discovered they were evenly matched. Perhaps the worst thing for the British forces to discover however was how much ammunition was needed to sustain a real shooting war.

Napoleon may have had a problem with food, the British discovered they had a problem with artillery shells. In combat an artillery battery fired shells at a prodigious rate. The army which had landed in France in 1914 carried with it just enough shells to enable it to be engaged in continuous action for no more than two days: that was just the tiniest fraction of shells needed to sustain a war for a few months, let alone keep the guns firing for years.

By the start of 1915 it was becoming obvious that the war would be a long one, and that the country had not been ready for such extended hostilities. Most critically, insufficient provision had been made for battles in which days-long artillery barrages

Above, both pictures: *Scenes in the factory during the first world war.* ***Right:*** *Stockyard personnel at the National Projectile Factory,(Birtley) in 1917.*

known as National Projectile Factories. Workers' wages would be paid by the Government; the factory managers would be paid by the contractors.

Not surprisingly the North East was considered to be an excellent location to build munitions factories. The region already had an engineering and chemical industry; there was coal to provide power and nearby iron and steel works. It was also safe from German aircraft which were by then just beginning to extend their range across the channel. In July 1915 an agreement was reached with Armstrong-Whitworth to build two factories at Birtley. One of the factories would make shells and the other cartridge cases. Refugee Belgians had already been successfully employed at Armstrong-Whitworth's Elswick works. In August an agreement was reached to also employ Belgians at Birtley

would be a dominant feature. The British army was being seriously let down by British industry.

By the first Spring of the war the 'Shell Scandal' had brought down Herbert Asquith's Liberal Government. The new coalition government, curiously still with Asquith at its head, immediately established a new Ministry of Munitions, appointing the former Chancellor of the Exchequer, Welshman and future Prime Minister David Lloyd George, to lead it.

The dynamic Lloyd George put all his energy into raising munitions production to meet the insatiable demand. But even with his indefatigable efforts the situation could not be changed quickly. Even by the summer factory output was still falling far short of the quantities needed.

It became obvious that if the Government's own armaments factories couldn't meet the demand then production would have to be contracted out. An agreement was reached in which the Government agreed to pay the cost of building factories which private contractors would build and manage. These new entities would be

Some 4,000 workers would be needed, and a firm of Belgian engineers was contracted to recruit that number from amongst the refugees. Unhappily very few of the Belgians stepped forward. The Belgian Government in exile, based in London, was contacted and asked to assist. An agreement being reached between the British and the Belgians in February 1916 in which the Belgian administration agreed to manage the factories and provide the labour whilst the British Government agreed to meet all expenses. A British Liaison Administrator together with an administrative staff, took responsibility for such things as wages and the purchase of raw materials and supplies.

Top left: *Shells awaiting despatch to France during World War I.* ***Right:*** *Belgian workers on the production line circa 1917.*

Originally it had been intended that the Belgians would work and live with English workers, but a thousand Belgian soldiers could not be easily billeted in local homes. It was quickly decided to build houses for all the Belgians. The houses formed a complete village 'Elisabethville'. The new village was laid out on model lines with hostels for the single men and cottages for families: 667 two and three-bedroomed houses were built.

As the workers from the Army were still soldiers they remained under military discipline. Whatever their job they were soldiers first and foremost, having to wear uniform both at work and outside the camp. Belgian civilians however remained under the jurisdiction of English civil law. The village however was administered under military law by the exiled Belgian Government; there were no British bobbies in sight - a Belgian officer, assisted by a force of gendarmes, kept order.

But the Belgian influx did not simply include soldiers and munitions workers. The local Post Office, although it was British, was staffed by Belgian officials. Belgian doctors, assisted by Belgian nurses and nuns, ran a hospital; Belgian teachers staffed a school; and Belgian priests looked after the church and cemetery. Even the village shop was managed by Belgians.

The National Projectile Factory was closed down in 1918 at the end of the first world war; part of it was sold off to local industrialists whilst what remained was mothballed against future need. As soon as conditions in their own country made it possible for them to return the Belgian

As a result of this arrangement Armstrong-Whitworth now handed over control of its shell factory, though it retained control of the cartridge case factory. The shell factory began production in the summer of 1916. Deliveries of six-inch high explosive shells began in July 1916, 60 pounder shrapnel shells were leaving the factory by the end of August and eight-inch explosive shells at the end of September. Other types of shell would also be produced. At last Lloyd George had some good news to report, but it had taken more than a year for the 'Shell Scandal' to be resolved.

Meanwhile since the Belgian civilian volunteers were still not coming forward in sufficient numbers to meet demand the possibility of using Belgian soldiers was raised. As a result a thousand men were withdrawn from the Belgian Army, whilst those wounded who had been discharged from hospital would be examined in the hope of employing them in the munitions factories also.

Top left: *English and Belgian workers pictured in 1918.* ***Above left:*** *Shell production in 1916.* ***Right:*** *Birtley products, 1916.*

workers and their families were repatriated, inevitably however a few, enamoured of the area, and enamoured of some of its inhabitants, remained and settled locally.

Around 1920 Sir William Angus & Co Ltd took over some of the premises and began to assemble the now long forgotten Angus Sanderson Tourer motor car on the site.

Elisabethville continued to exist until shortly before the outbreak of the second world war, when it was torn down. The school however remained in use for many decades afterwards. Other homes have since been erected where the Belgian village once stood but the area is still referred to by locals as Elisabethville. Today a few unusual surnames in the telephone directory, and the cemetery, with its 13 war graves, are some of the few remaining reminders of the many Belgians who made their homes here during the Great War of 1914-18.

And that could have been the end of the story, but of course it was not. Clouds were gathering over Europe. In 1933 Adolph Hitler, the leader of the Nazi party became Chancellor of Germany. In 1936 Hitler reoccupied the Rhineland and formed an alliance, or Axis as it later became known, with Mussolini the Italian fascist leader. Later that year both Hitler and Mussolini would give their support to General Franco the soon-to-be victorious leader of Spain's fascist forces in the Spanish Civil War.

It was not yet time for Britain to enter a new war with Germany, but the signs were not promising. Prime Minister Chamberlain had not yet flown to Munich and returned with that famous and worthless piece of paper signed by Hitler promising 'peace in our time'. That notorious incident would not occur until 1938. In the meantime someone in the Government was quietly following yet another important maxim 'those who seek peace should prepare for war'.

Early in 1936, with commendable foresight, it was decided to reactivate the factory at Birtley to supplement those in Woolwich, Enfield and Waltham Abbey. Some of the buildings at Birtley which had been sold off were now bought back, and new plant for cartridge case and shell-making was bought and installed. Peter Brown was the first man to be employed when the factory reopened in 1936: he would stay there until 1974 after completing 38 years of service. The plant which had been under care and maintenance between the wars was reconditioned and the factory reopened officially for production in 1937, and was ready for war in 1939. Expansion continued, and at its peak of production during the second world war employed some 5,500 women and 2,000 men. By 1943 more than 40 Royal Ordnance factories were employing 300,000 men and women.

After World War II ended in 1945 output was reduced to cater for a reduction in demand for ammunition. The

Top: *The King presenting the BEM to M Bradley, Convenor of shop stewards AEU, June 1941.* ***Below:*** *J J Lawson MP enjoys a cup of tea after opening the new canteen, February 1942.* ***Right:*** *A 1920 Angus Sanderson Tourer. Sir William Angus Sanderson & Co Ltd assembled motor cars on the factory site between 1918 and 1920.*

a 14 year old earning the grand sum of 8/6d for a 48 hour week: Lawrence would not retire until 1987 after a record-breaking 50 years and 3 months of unbroken service.

Today the United Kingdom's Ministry of Defence remains the main customer for Birtley's output. Its products have been developed and greatly improved upon over the years - though they still consist of shell, anti-tank shot and cartridge cases, all of which would be used extensively in the Falklands, the Gulf War of 1991 and in the conflict with Iraq in 2003.

Attlee government retained 21 of the wartime ROFs, allowing them to diversify into civilian production, but retaining a strategic reserve of munitions skills. Plant was installed at Birtley for the manufacture of steel houses. That project did not get far however and the plant was then turned over to the manufacture of office furniture. At the outbreak of the Korean war in 1951 the plant again reverted to ammunition production, an activity which has continued to the present day. In 1969 the neighbouring CWS Tinplate works was acquired, the site then consisted of 32 acres, its largest extent ever.

In 1985 Royal Ordnance was privatised, two years later it was acquired by British Aerospace. As a result of the end of the Cold War and the reduction in the requirements of the UK's armed forces the former CWS site was sold off in 1997.

Over the decades many people in the area have worked at the 'ROF'. Some folk have worked there all their working lives: Dennis Lightfoot for example, who was awarded an OBE for services to the defence industry, retired in 1989 after 47 years continuous service; and Lawrence Taggart who was employed in 1937 as

Top left and left: *The Queen watches the examination of cartridge cases by disabled ex-servicemen and discusses work with a female machine operator, June 1941.* ***Below left:*** *Peter Brown being introduced to HRH Prince Philip during his visit to the factory on 10th May, 1972.* ***Below:*** *Shell's and cartridge cases made at Birtley in use during the Iraq conflict in 2003.*

Photograph by Reuters/Stephen Hird

A driving ambition

What would one day become Murray Hogg Ltd began its operations on 1st April 1928. The business was founded by 22 year old Murray Hogg from Cumberland; he was a young man who had until then worked on farms, and in the timber business, working for relatives.

The reason for Murray's move to Newcastle was his wife Jane, known to all as Jenny. Her parents' youngest child, Jenny had moved to Cumberland with her parents when they had retired; however, the country life didn't suit them and they moved back to Newcastle. Murray, at first unable to find suitable employment in Newcastle, followed them a little later.

It was now that Murray bought his first vehicle, a Chevrolet, from a Jesmond haulier for which he paid £90. It was a brave move, since although Murray owned a motorcycle he was unable to drive a lorry!

Quickly mastering the problem of how to drive his purchase Murray's small transport business prospered as he bought and sold sand, gravel and coal.

But more investment was needed. Murray asked his father for a loan of £300 to buy a new Bedford lorry. Murray's father was an LNER employee and had some shares in the railway. When he went to cash in some of his shares to raise the money the LNER official asked why he wanted such a large sum of money; on explaining that it was for a lorry they were aghast saying 'What and set up in competition against us!'

The investment was a good one, despite the views of the LNER. By the outbreak of the Second World War in 1939 the business had six vehicles on the road and seven employees.

Until 1935 the firm had been operating from rented premises in Bowsden Terrace, South Gosforth but had then moved to new premises in Fawdon. A garage was built there to house four vehicles.

At Fawdon the Hogg family became the hub of the small village, starting a taxi business there in 1937, which amongst other things had the contract for transferring cash from both the Midland bank and from Martins (now Barclays) - there was no Securicor in those days. In 1943 the Hogg family also bought the village shop, which Jenny ran, and the petrol filling station.

***Above right:** Jenny and Murray Hogg outside their village shop, 1954.* ***Right:** The premises at Bowsden Terrace, in 1953.*

By then the family was growing, with two sons and a daughter. Murray was born in 1934, Jim the following year and Nancy in 1940; a third son Colin, arrived in 1944. All three sons would eventually join their father in the family business.

Murray missed serving in the war, having lost an index finger in an accident at a timber mill several years previously; however, he still did his bit, carrying out duties as a special constable throughout the war.

Top: *A 5-ton Austin loaded with pit chucks, 1946.*
Above: *Murray junior's A35 van in front of a 1-tonner loaded with boxes for Marconi at Gateshead in 1959.*

At the outbreak of war in 1939 two of Murray Hogg's Bedford lorries had been commandeered for the war effort, but they were returned to him to carry out war work. Throughout the war the firm was involved in airfield construction for the War Department as well as being employed by the LNER to carry food from goods stations.

Until the outbreak of war the fleet had been added to with a new vehicle acquired every year. But between 1939 and 1945 no vehicles were released to civilians. After the war however,, Murray was issued with three new lorries: a Bedford, a Morris and a Commer: Murray swapped the latter two for Bedfords as soon as he could, that being his favourite make of trucks at the time.

Murray's first customer had been Carmichael & Harwood, a firm of jobbing builders located in the next yard to where the first vehicle was bought. Clark Taylor & Co. was another early client.

The first big customer however, was the building firm of Cussins. Unhappily the contract was lost for a while because the vehicles were being used on site clearance: as no excavating equipment was available a chain was attached to the lorry to pull up tree roots. Murray was so concerned about the damage which might be done to the vehicles he took them off the contract. Other early customers included local councils, Gosforth Urban District Council, Newcastle Corporation and Northumberland County Council. The firm would still be providing services to some of its earliest customers in the 21st century, clients such as Winthrop pharmaceutical laboratories, Scott Turner, Tyneside

aircrew but was unable to do so because of colour blindness; instead of spending his time in the air young Murray was placed in the RAF's motor section and spent two years in Iraq protecting oil pipelines and taking convoys through the desert.

Murray returned to Newcastle in 1954 and, now aged 20 began the process of building up the business at a time when his father was starting to look towards retirement.

By the time of Murray's return from National Service the firm had six vehicles on the road and he began to press for building up long distance delivery work, a proposal which came to fruition in 1955. The following year Jim returned from Malaysia where he had been sent to serve out his period of National Service and now joined the firm as a driver.

Third son, Colin, joined the firm in 1960 after a period working for a Commercial firm Buists as a mechanic.

The three brothers, Murray, Jim and Colin formed a partnership in 1967. Murray took on the role of Managing Director and oversaw all aspects of the business; Jim looked after warehousing whilst

Tinprinters - subsequently Sanofi Synthelabo - and Thomas Hedley which later became part of Proctor & Gamble.

By the 21st century long distance haulage would be a major element of business. The firm's first long distance job however, was carried out in 1942 for a lady from Gosforth whose daughter, family and furniture was in Liverpool. The task was to collect the daughter's furniture and take it to Gosforth for safety. The bombing in Liverpool was so bad however, that the lorry had to wait for two days to get into Liverpool before the driver could enter the city to collect his load.

By 1951 the premises at Fawdon had become too small and the premises at South Gosforth, which had been rented, were now bought and Bowsden Terrace became the hub of the whole business.

Murray joined his father in 1951; shortly afterwards however,, he had to do his National Service which he spent in the RAF, he had wanted to be selected as

Top left: *One of the firm's vehicles delivering one of Newcastle Aero Club's planes to the club following an accident.* ***Right:*** *One of the firm's vehicles in 1959.*

Colin became the fleet engineer, taking charge of vehicle maintenance.

By that time Murray's wife, Moira, had already been working for the firm for ten years, looking after the company accounts: she became Company Secretary following Jenny's death in 1984. However, until the firm had moved to a new site at North Gosforth Moira had to work from home since the Bowsden Terrace garage didn't have a ladies' toilet.

In these years Murray Hogg did everything he could to expand the business; when driving a lorry he would always wear a shirt and tie under his work clothes making it possible for him to go into offices where he was delivering in order to make new contacts and get new business.

That tenacity and enterprise worked; the business did grow. But the premises at Bowsden Terrace could only house eight vehicles and so in 1971 a new depot was built at Sandy Lane, North Gosforth; this gave more scope for expansion, it was able to house the ever growing fleet whilst also allowing for diversification into warehousing.

Company founder, Murray Hogg senior, died in 1972 at the age of 66; happily he lived to see the new depot open, having already seen the business he founded grow tenfold since he had bought his first vehicle in 1928.

The firm had until then continued to operate as a partnership, but in 1974, acting on legal advice, a limited company was formed, though at the time Murray Hogg Ltd was used only for the warehousing arm of the business - a situation which would persist until 1995.

At North Gosforth a further warehouse was built, and the land adjoining it was bought in 1976. In 1984 the neighbouring Rowntree Mackintosh site came up for sale, and that too was bought by the company. The business now occupied a site of some 10 acres in a prime location between the A1 and the A19.

The increasingly large fleet of Murray Hogg lorries became a familiar sight in the North East. In the early days tipper lorries had been used but by 1973, due to the changing nature of work, tippers were no longer needed. The advent of the articulated vehicle made the fleet a lot more flexible, since any 'tractor unit' could be used to pull any trailer. The first articulated vehicle had been bought in 1973 and was driven by Jeff Hays, someone who would still be driving for the company into the 21st century.

Until then the firm's fleet had been mainly made up of Leyland lorries but due to superior performance and the greater availability of spare parts a decision was taken to switch to more reliable Mercedes Benz. By the 1990s the company

***Top left:** Murray Hogg senior enjoying retirement in his 1964 Singer Gazelle. **Right:** The firm's vintage lorry appearing at a rally in the Isle of Man with Colin Hogg senior.*

would be almost all Mercedes - and so many had been bought over the years that Murray was presented with an award at the Savoy Hotel in London in 1995 by Mercedes for being one of its best customers.

In 1986 the company diversified further when North East Vehicle Movements, a car transportation business, was acquired. The name was changed to Vehicle Movements (NE) Ltd and began with three vehicles; today it runs 23.

Though the company continues to operate a large number of Mercedes vehicles, by the end of the century it also had introduced Volvos, a make of vehicle more suited to the car transporter trailers used in the firm's Vehicle Movements operation; Scanias too were introduced to enable comparison to be made.

But not everything was a success: for a short time, beginning in 1990, the firm also sold fuel, running two tankers, but this part of the business was sold in 1993.

As the business grew the third generation of the family joined the company: Jim's son, Murray, began working in the traffic office in 1981.

In 1982 Colin Junior joined his father Colin in running the workshops and his brother David, arrived in 1987 and also worked in the maintenance section before moving to look after warehousing in 1997 on Jim Hogg's retirement.

Colin Hogg's youngest son, Paul, joined the firm in 1991, working mainly in the Vehicle Movements side of the business.

The Company appreciated the importance of the quality standard and in 1992 received accreditation to BS5750. This has subsequently been upgraded over the years to the latest standard, BS EN ISO 9001:2000.

Murray Hogg and his wife Moira retired in 1998, though they continued to take an active interest in the business, being kept up to date by their daughter Alyson.

Alyson, Murray and Moira's elder daughter had joined the business in 1995 and took over the role of company accountant when Moira retired in 1998.

In 1999 all the founder's grandchildren were made directors of the two companies: Murray Hogg Ltd and Vehicle Movements NE Ltd.

Top left and above right: *Loading and storing stock in the firm's extensive warehouse facilities.* ***Right:*** *An aerial view of the site.*

Without a doubt, part of the secret of Murray Hogg's success lies in its ability to move with the times. The family which little more than 75 years ago relied on one vehicle for its livelihood is today the proprietor of a large, modern haulage and car transportation fleet, extensive warehousing and property portfolio. And though the company keeps a sharp eye on the future it also honours its past: the company still has an old Austin which is displayed at vintage vehicle shows, after having been restored to its full glory in Murray Hogg's state of the art workshops.

Alyson is in charge of accounts, Murray is Managing Director and takes care of traffic, Colin is fleet engineer in charge of the workshops, David manages warehousing and Paul takes care of car transportation.

By the opening years of the 21st century the company had 114 staff and was running a fleet of around 100 vehicles ranging from small vans to 44 tonne tractor units. The present generation of directors are closely involved with everything and continue to look for new opportunities. Most recently the business has adapted to changes in the transport industry by joining an overnight pallet network providing an even more efficient and flexible service. In 2002 seven vehicles and 15 trailers would be based in Yorkshire to service a major radiator and boiler manufacturer.

Sadly Jim Hogg passed away in 2002, having retired in 1997, however, later that year his grandson Christopher Hogg, the Murray's youngest son, joined the company and began learning the business in 2002.

Essentially however, Murray Hogg has remained a family-run firm with its roots in the local community, from which its loyal workforce is, and will continue to be drawn. The company is deservedly proud of its success, but equally it takes great pleasure in its record of providing secure employment for generations of local people - ever since the business was started, all those years ago by Murray Hogg.

Top left: *One of Murray Hogg's articulated lorries alongside one of the fleet of car transporters.* ***Left:*** *One of the firm's newest vehicles with an airbrushed illustration of past lorries on the side.* ***Below:*** *The current directors from left to right: Colin Hogg, David Hogg, Alyson Hogg, Paul Hogg and Murray Hogg.*

Homes of our own

There are many things that contribute to the sum of human happiness. Owning your own home is high on the list, but then so is getting a decent rate of interest on our spare money. Building Societies have been helping folk achieve these twin aims for a very long time indeed.

Mortgages - loans made against property - have been around for centuries, but mortgages for ordinary people were very much a product of the Victorian era; and an outcome of the Victorians' obsession with self improvement.

Most Building Societies today have dropped the word 'permanent' from their names but readers will readily recall that the word featured prominently in the names of most societies not too many years ago. But in the very early days of building societies most were not 'permanent'.

The idea of an 'impermanent' building society may seem odd but the original idea was to establish a society whose members would collectively save their money to buy homes for themselves: when all the members had paid for their homes then the society would be wound up.

Above: *An interest-calculating digital accounting machine used in the early 1960s.* ***Below:*** *Grainger & Percy Building Society's General Office, Newcastle, c1960.* ***Right:*** *Crude technology in the early 1960s, an addressograph printing machine.*

Some building societies however became permanent, that is to say they continued in existence indefinitely, attracting new members: investors and those seeking mortgages.

Today, when the majority of people either have a mortgage, have had one, or hope to have one, it's hard to believe that not too long ago the vast majority of working folk rented their homes and could scarcely imagine becoming members of the propertied classes. But the impetus for what would become a massive wave of social change began with philanthropically minded people in the middle of the 19th century, not least with the founders of bodies such as what would eventually become today's Newcastle Building Society.

Central to this was the concept of mutuality, which in simple terms means the members are also the owners. By adopting this guiding principle building societies act in the best interest of their members, rather than other groups such as share

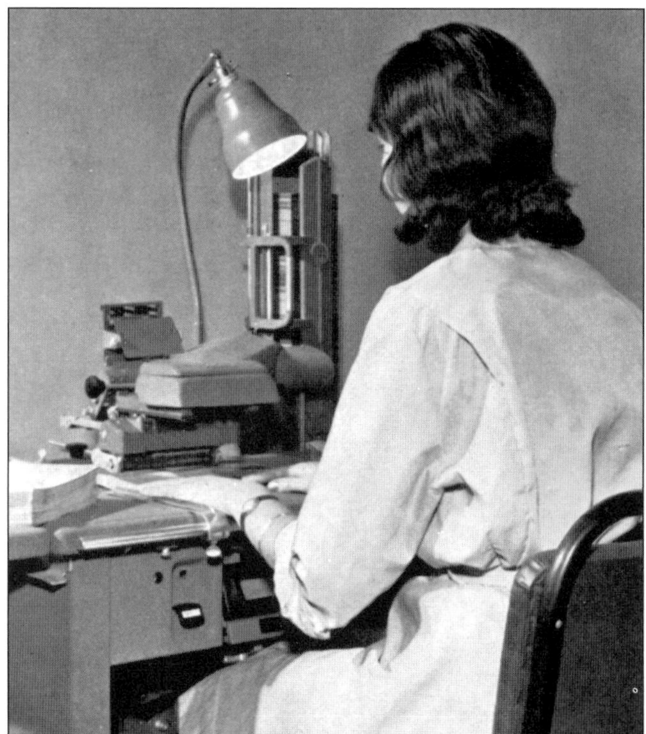

holders in a private company. Newcastle Building Society has always been totally committed to mutuality, and remains so today. By doing so it believes it can offer the best value to its members over the long term.

By the opening decade of the 21st century the Newcastle Building Society, with roots going back to 1861, had become the biggest building society based in the North East with a current network of 51 branches stretching from Falkirk to Gibraltar and with a strong innovative product range and with assets which placed it amongst the industry's top 13 societies.

Today's Newcastle Building Society was formed on 1st July 1980 by the merger of the Grainger and Newcastle upon Tyne Permanent Building Societies. At that time the combined assets of the two societies were £150 million: the assets of the Grainger at 31st December 1979 having been £63.9 million and the Newcastle Permanent £84.3 million.

The Grainger Permanent Benefit Building Society was established in 1863, its first offices being in Westgate Road: in the first year of business £22,177 was lent on mortgages the first advance being a mortgage of £170 on a house in Middle Street, Newcastle at a rate of three per cent. To put this into context gross lending in the first six months of 2003 was £331 million.

The name of the Society was chosen to perpetuate the name of Richard Grainger, the celebrated builder who played a conspicuous part in the development and improvement of Newcastle.

Up until 1866 all loans made were required to be repaid within 12 months, but that year the maximum term was increased to 20 years. Interest rates increased significantly around this period rising to five per cent, and then to seven and a half per cent. Despite those rises demand for loans continued to grow apace. By 1882 'the Grainger's' assets would reach £233,392.

The Grainger took a 'transfer of engagements' of the Tynemouth United Star Bowkett Building Society in 1913. Even so the first world war of 1914-18 led to some reduction in assets.

In 1928 the Head Office was moved to the Royal Exchange Buildings in Hood Street and by 1948, despite a virtual cessation of business during the second world war, assets had increased to £2 million.

***Top right:** The Hood Street Banking Hall in 1958.* ***Left and above left:** The Whickham branch both before and after conversion.*

During the second world war the Society had taken over the City of Newcastle Building Society, and in 1946, a year after the war's end, had taken over those of the Northumberland Building Society too. The ending of the war was the start of a period of unprecedented economic growth. Harold Macmillan truthfully said at the end of the 1950s that we had never had it so good. That sustained prosperity led many young working folk to start buying their homes.

In 1957 the Grainger merged with the Percy Building Society to form the Grainger and Percy Building Society: the assets of the merged Society were £7 million. That same year the Society moved into newly constructed premises in Hood Street.

Founded in 1865 the roots and policies of the Percy Building Society were much the same as the Grainger. The Chairman of the Percy at the time of the merger was Colonel RP Winter, the grandson of JM Winter and the son of Robert P Winter who had been successive Secretaries of the Grainger from 1871 until 1926.

Top left: *Grainger Building Society's motorised moveable deed storage in the strong room in the 1960s.* ***Right:*** *Grainger & Percy Building Society Literature from the late 50s and early 60s through to 2003.*

In 1974 there was a further 'Transfer of Engagements', this time from the Victory Building Society in South Shields.

The Society changed its name to the Grainger Building Society in 1975.

The Newcastle Upon Tyne Permanent Building Society was established in December 1861 by George Brewis and Thomas Strachan with the stated aims of 'by mutual co-operation to enable the members to acquire property and to supply to the saving classes a safe means of realising a good interest'.

'The Newcastle' held its first meeting at Mr Baker's temperance hotel in Westgate Street. In its first year of business the Society advanced £36,588 10s 1d on 581 'awards' as loans were then known. For some years the 'NPBS' would be the only building society in the area.

In its early years the Society had no permanent home and Annual General Meetings were held at the Temperance Hotel in Westgate Street, The Royal Arcade and The Temperance Hall in Nelson Street. In 1871 the Society opened permanent offices in Central Buildings, Grainger Street West. By 1920 the Society's assets exceeded £1 million and had doubled again by 1928.

In 1942 the North Eastern Permanent Building Society transferred its engagements to the Newcastle followed in 1961 by the Portland Building Society, and in 1979 the St Andrew's Building Society did likewise.

Despite these mergers 'the Newcastle' still remained firmly based in the city with no aim of expanding its services. Only in 1960, after almost a century in business, did the Newcastle Upon Tyne Building Society buy

premises in Carlisle with a view to opening its first branch - it was to be a foretaste of things to come, though many hurdles would need to be mounted before the modern Society would emerge. Arguably personalities as much as financial imperatives would be the key to change.

Throughout many decades of the Society's existence the Heppell family had been deeply involved with its management. Mr John Heppell had become Secretary of the Society in 1888 starting a long family association with the Society. In 1945 John Heppell's son, P Forsyth Heppell, was elected Chairman and in his turn his son, PWE Heppell, became Chairman in March 1966 remaining Chairman until October 1987 by which time his son, JW Heppell had already joined the board.

Another key figure in developing the modern Newcastle upon Tyne Permanent Building Society was Tom Bathurst. He joined the 'NPBS' in December 1960, having previously worked for the Portman Building Society since leaving school and had, except for absence on war service, worked in the field ever since. He became the Newcastle Permanent Building Society's Chief Executive on 1st January 1961. At that time the Society was the second largest Building Society in the North East, the largest then being the Northern Counties Building Society. In the whole country in the early 1960s there were some 200 building societies registered, although some 60 of them were in fact 'dormant' whilst the rest were operating with varying degrees of activity. Despite luke-warm enthusiasm for growth the Society still opened its first branch in Carlisle in 1961 - the first salvo in what would result in massive change.

The NPBS installed its own computer in the early 1970s, at a cost exceeding one million pounds (a huge amount in those days). The computer filled a whole room in the Society.

On 31st December 1980 the Newcastle Permanent Building Society amalgamated with the Grainger Building Society, creating the Newcastle Building Society. Following amalgamation Tom Bathurst, became Joint Chief Executive alongside the former Chief Executive of the Grainger Building Society, staying in that role until he retired in 1981. Bill Midgley was employed by the Society in 1978 as Assistant General Manager and became Chief Executive in November 1986. Following his retirement in July 1998, Robert Hollinshead became Chief Executive. Robert joined the Society in 1992 as Finance Director and became Operations Director in early 1997 before taking over the reins the following year. Robert has been instrumental in the development of the Society's technology systems and in helping the Society establish a reputation for offering innovative and ground breaking products.

***Top left:** Tom Bathurst, Chief Executive of the Newcastle Permanent Building Society from 1961. **Left:** Grainger & Percy's building on Hood Street, Newcastle, which opened on 6th January, 1958. **Below:** Robert Hollinshead, Chief Executive of Newcastle Building Society.*

Supporting Robert in this forward thinking approach is the Society's current Chairman, Chris Hilton, a Senior Partner with Eversheds law firm in Newcastle.

In June 1991, the Society convinced the City that 54 New Bridge Street, the BBC's old Broadcasting House would make a great centre-piece for their new headquarters. In 1994, after three years construction work to completely renovate and refurbish the building, the headquarters were complete. The Society named the building Portland House in recognition of the original row of houses named Portland Place and of the Portland Pub which replaced them.

HRH Princess Margaret officially opened Portland House in November 1994. The BBC's old Broadcasting House is now the Society's executive suite, the jewel in the crown of head office.

Some readers may remember that the old building at the centre of Portland House began life as the Newcastle Maternity Hospital. Built in 1826 to provide maternity care for impoverished married women it had become, by around 80 years old a rest room for the unemployed, paid for by the Church Army. Hundreds of men would use it each day for games, reading and cheap refreshments. It later became BBC radio and TV studios.

'The Newcastle' developed the latest technology to link its branches with its head office ensuring a fast efficient service for its mortgage, investment and pensions clientele. The 1990s would also be the decade when the Society's assets passed the billion pound mark, a landmark passed in 1992 with great celebration.

The 1990s was of course a decade of change in what had by now become known as the financial services industry. Banks began to compete in the field of mortgages whilst a number of building societies chose to become banks, with shares traded on the stock market.

But regardless of whether or not they became banks all building societies need to move with the times in an ever more competitive market place for their services. As a result the range of 'financial products' and the advice on offer would become increasingly more sophisticated as time passed. And the Newcastle Building Society was not going to be left on the sidelines: the sleepy days of yore when board members and senior staff could comfortably ignore innovation and enterprise were very much part of history.

In 2002, the Newcastle developed a system of 'Virtualisation' which means they can utilise highly skilled staff based throughout the Society's network at any one time - whether that be in head office, the branches or even working from home. Today, whether customers contact the Society by phone or written correspondence, their enquiries are immediately routed to appropriately skilled staff throughout the Society's network, ensuring a more rapid and efficient service. Newcastle Building Society was also one of the first to launch an Online Savings Account and the first to utilise Digital TV.

Top right: *HRH Princess Margaret opening Newcastle Building Society's head office, Portland House, in November 1994.* ***Above right:*** *The Hood Street Branch after its facelift in 2003.* ***Left:*** *21st century technology in the Customer Contact Centre.*

In 2002, the Society was recognised as the Best Large Company in Tyne & Wear for investing in people and in the same year also won Gold in the Investors in People (IIP) Outstanding Practice Awards. At the 2003 Financial Sector Technology (FST) Awards, the Society won 'Most Innovative Use of Customer Relation Management (CRM)' and 'Best Use of Contact Centres'.

As well as installing the latest technology the Society has embarked on a major branch refurbishment programme. In November 2002, Auf Wiedersehen Pet star, Tim Healy, helped the Society say goodbye to the old, and hello to the new when he officially re-opened the Gosforth branch after a major refurbishment and unveiled the Society's new logo. The new logo more accurately reflects the Society's position as a modern and innovative financial institution, moving away from the black and white, to a fresh, new green and blue logo. In keeping with the traditional values of the Society, it kept the strong image of the castle, but the more vibrant colours represented a 'new look with old values'.

Despite it's size the Society is very much committed to the local community and in 1992 The Newcastle Building Society Community Fund was set up; each year £100,000 is donated to worthy charities in the areas surrounding the branches. The three main objectives of the fund are to promote training and learning for people of all ages, to nurture and encourage new talent and to improve the quality of life in local communities. The Society also launched the Members' Community Fund in 2003, whereby members can choose to make an annual donation from their savings to a charity which either supports children's education, adult literature and numeracy or IT schemes for the over 55s.

Newcastle Building Society has come a long way since the first shoots emerged in 1861. Over the past 140 years it has built itself up into one of the strongest mutuals in the UK. It can now look forward with confidence to the next 140 years.

Top left: *A bird's eye view of Portland House in 2003.* ***Above:*** *Newcastle Building Society staff Maxine Lindsay, Phil Grand, Colin Greaves, Chris Shaw and Shirley Briggs with the FST Awards presented to the Society in 2003.* ***Above right:*** *Tim Healy, with Steven Marks (Assistant General Manager), opens the new look Gosforth branch in November 2002.* ***Right:*** *Chief Executive, Robert Hollinshead, pictured outside the new look Gosforth branch in 2002.*

Moving the earth

It's not much fun trying to dig a hole in the ground with a pick and shovel. And it's even less fun if there's more rock than earth to be shifted. But until the 20th century hand tools were mostly what was used for the laborious work of moving earth and rock in the construction industry. Though today enormous mechanical diggers may effortlessly create our motorways and by-passes just spare a thought for those armies of poor navvies who built our railway cuttings and embankments with shovels, pickaxes and wheelbarrows - and before the railways they did the same to build the canals. If only they could have seen today's powerful earth-moving equipment.

Though steam power was used for moving earth and rock in the 19th century it was the early years of the 20th which witnessed the start of a revolution which continues to this day. Between 1904 and 1914 the Americans showed how it could be done when they used massive steam powered cranes and excavators to claw out the 50 mile length of the Panama Canal.

It would however not be until after the second world war that caterpillar-tracked mobile cranes and excavators would become an everyday sight in Britain and a familiar feature of every building site.

But excavators bring their own problems. At times whatever is at the end of an excavator's powerful arm needs to be changed: often because being quite literally at the sharp end of operations, they inevitably get damaged - but equally it is often simply to change the type of attachment.

Over the passing decades since the end of World War II the growth in the use of various attachments to the arms of hydraulic excavators has not been matched by the ease with which they could be changed. Talk to any excavator operator in the 1970s and one of his biggest complaints would have been the time-consuming, and invariably, frustrating business of having to remove and replace metal pins when changing from bucket to bucket or from bucket to rock breaker. Happily a time would come when excavators operators would be able to quickly change attachments without even the need to climb out of their cabs.

Above: *A young Gary Miller inside a face shovel bucket repaired by his own fair hand.* ***Right:*** *The first UH 261 sold by the UK Hitachi dealer in the early 1990s, equipped with a Miller purpose-built rock bucket.* ***Below:*** *Men at work on a Marrion face shovel refurbishment.*

Though several makes of quick coupler would eventually appear on the market, one which would offer unique advantages is produced in Newcastle upon Tyne by Miller (UK) Ltd.

Miller UK Ltd, founded in the late 1970s to service the construction and quarrying industries, has since developed into one of Europe's leading bucket and coupler manufacturers, supplying its product range to customers across the globe.

From the firm's first bucket (made in 1979 for National Smokeless Fuels at Lampton Coke Works) the business has enjoyed a continual increase in demand for products exclusively designed and manufactured by its employees. For more than a quarter of a century now the name Miller has been synonymous within the industry for its honest, no nonsense approach to its business - mainly because its representatives have consistently listened to customers' demands and provided products that offer value for money, as well as an investment opportunity.

That philosophy has been combined with the company's mission statement: 'To be recognised as the premier bucket and coupler manufacturer world wide'. That combination has helped the company to become universally recognised as an expert in its field. But where did it all start?

In 1978 a keen young man left his safe job and started out on his own, offering an on-site mobile welding service to local quarries, mines, open cast coal sites and plant hire companies. The boss of the welding company he had left told the young Keith Miller, 'There's no real chance of promotion in the foreseeable future', but also generously added, 'Your job is always here if you go bust'. There was however, not much chance of Keith going bust.

It didn't take Keith Miller, then just 21, long to secure a regular stream of work from the North East's construction industry - not least an important contract to maintain the plant at the Kielder Dam project in Northumberland. 'I knew I was a good welder' Keith would recall. 'Many customers asked for me by name; or the tall skinny lad as I was back then. After canvassing a few of them I decided I could make a living even if I didn't have a van. I sold my precious Starsky & Hutch style Ford Granada and purchased a second hand Ford Escort estate car which cost £295 from a local auction'. This solved the transport problem and along with a Mighty Midgit welding set, Keith was in business.

By the end of 1979 demand for the young engineer's services had grown to a point where his brother Gary was called in to join him.

Top left: *Jacqui Miller presenting 'the most couplers sold' award throughout France to its first official distributor.* ***Above left:*** *The early days, Miller on site and ready for action.* ***Right:*** *The first bucket export order secured from the first Miller workshop, Tower Street, Newcastle.*

With their strong work ethic and will to succeed the pair soon offered a 24-hour a day, seven days a week service. To keep up with demand the duo soon found themselves having to employ a small team of local welders and fabricators, and a new name for themselves: Miller Welding Engineers.

Along with that early success came the need for extra working space and a factory was acquired at Tower Street, Newcastle.

By 1981 the Miller brothers had switched their focus, from simple welding repairs, to the manufacture of buckets for hydraulic excavators and for wheeled loading shovels: now for the first time the company exhibited their products at the National Exhibition Centre in Birmingham, which was attended by Keith, Gary and their 17 year old sister Jacqui.

At the exhibition the Millers were successful in obtaining some substantial enquiries from outside their native North East.

Orders for the company's products now came in from all over the country. As a result Jacqui Miller now joined her brothers on a full-time basis, helping promote the Miller name throughout the construction industry. As a result of increasing sales a move was made to larger premises in Newcastle's Skinnerburn Road where there was enough workshop space to meet the needs imposed by an ever-increasing order book.

During the following years not only did demand continue to rise from the construction sector, but sales now began to grow to the quarry and mining sectors, as well as the company offering bucket and attachment repairs to all the well-known makes of earth moving equipment.

Above: *Keith, Jacqui and Gary Miller attending their first International Exhibition in Paris, France.*
Below: *Skinnerburn Road, a hive of activity!*

By the middle of the 1980s the three Millers had realised how important it was to raise the company's business profile through advertising and other marketing activities.

Ways of promoting the business included attending exhibitions, sending out mailshots, telephoning potential customers, as well as advertising in the press.

It was as a result of attending an exhibition in 1988 that a partnership was established which changed the growing company's future direction remarkably.

As a result of contacts made at the exhibition the Miller company entered into a working relationship with a contracting company that was then developing the idea of a quick and efficient method of changing excavator buckets without the need for the operator to leave his cab.

The Quick Coupler concept originated in New Zealand, however, it was Keith and the team at Miller who developed the design and engineering and eventually introduced the first Quick Coupler to the market in 1989. This revolutionary method of changing buckets and attachments within seconds was capable of saving operators millions of hours in otherwise unproductive down time, and of course, in the process saving thousands of operators millions of pounds.

The big advantage of the quick coupler over some competitors' designs was that no alterations needed to be made to existing buckets or other attachments. Since then Miller has continuously improved the original design, therefore the company can today offer the world's only truly universal hydraulic coupler produced in a range of sizes to suit any type of excavator, bucket or attachment, and also work with buckets from different excavator brands from the same/similar tonnage category.

The hydraulic coupler was operated from a simple switch inside the excavator cab. The system allowed an experienced operator to change over from one attachment to another in less than half a minute. Even better, the system could be fitted to any excavator in only a few hours without the need to alter the machine's hydraulics system.

Though the typical cost then was around £3,500, plus fitting, the subsequent time savings were impressive. A busy machine carrying out a variety of work on a construction site might need to change attachments five or more times a day. Without a quick coupler that could mean an excavator driver spending up to two hours on the unproductive task of removing and refitting pins. By comparison, using an excavator fitted with a quick coupler, the operator would only have production disrupted for two and a half minutes each day - inevitably saving a great deal of time and money.

Above: *One of the very first Miller Quick Couplers.*
Right: *Buckets bound for export.*

With millions at stake not surprisingly demand for the Miller Quick Coupler soared. The company was soon able to invest in further product development, including making continuous improvements to the original design.

But for the Millers such small successes did not yet meet their aspirations. Having helped others become more productive they wanted to be more productive themselves: and for their firm to grow. In late 1991 the Millers were visited by the famous 'trouble-shooter' Sir John Harvey Jones who looked at the company's operation and gave them two pieces of advice 'Sort out your production flow' and 'Get into Europe'.
By the mid 1990s, armed with a business plan which called for production to treble in three years, the production flow problems were sorted out in a much larger factory and stockyard than the company had ever had before, and distributors had been taken on in Germany and Italy. Markets in Belgium, France and Spain would be next on the agenda.

In 1998 the company celebrated its 20th anniversary with a £1.75 million investment in new plant and machinery, expanding into a second factory at Blaydon in preparation for an anticipated surge in demand for its products and services, not least from the USA. The Millers were at CONEXPO held in March 1999 in Las Vegas, one of the most important and prestigious exhibitions in the world for the construction industry. As a result of rolling their business dice in Las Vegas a major contract with Caterpillar Inc of North America - the world's largest construction machine manufacturer - was secured.

Today the Miller company has contracts to supply famous names in excavator production all across the world, some examples being: Caterpillar, JCB, Komatsu, Case New Holland, Hitachi and Volvo.

Though at its outset the business may have been a one-man band, by the opening years of the 21st century the company was split into three divisions: Quick Coupler manufacture, hydraulic excavator bucket manufacture and a specialist products division. The specialist division is dedicated to offering bespoke solutions to individual customers own specifications anywhere in the world, in addition to managing the original repair and servicing of buckets and attachments.

The company is still run by its three early members. The Board comprises its Chairman, Keith Miller, the Technical Director Gary Miller and their younger sister Jacqui Miller who is the Sales and Marketing Director.

Top: *The Addison factory, acquired for the 90s expansion.* ***Above right:*** *Keith, Jacqui and Gary Miller with 'Troubleshooter' Sir John Harvey Jones.* ***Right:*** *Miller on site and at your service fully equipped for safer coupler installation.*

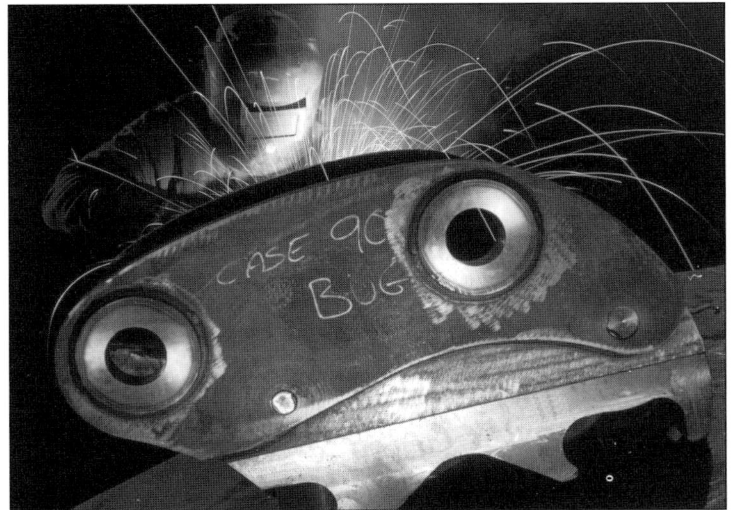

Volvo and with plans to expand into Asia and Australasia in the near future.

By the end of 2003 the Company will have completed another factory relocation to a significantly larger facility set in 18 acres of land in Cramlington just outside Newcastle. This will amalgamate all three existing production units under one roof and will not only further streamline the manufacturing processes but afford Miller the space to further expand to meet the Company's ambitious business plan.

How did they do it? The Millers put it down to a philosophy of following; 'The Three Ps' - people, products and performance. The right people ensure that the correct products are supplied which in turn perform to the customer's expectations. In pursuit of that philosophy the company has a continuing programme of staff training running alongside ongoing research directed specifically at developing new cost-effective products.

Those who once used picks and spades must have blessed the inventor of the mechanical shovel. Since those days excavator drivers must have equally often blessed the name of Miller.

The business continues to expand through continuing to improve its products and the introduction of novel solutions to help improve customers' productivity. One of the most recent of Miller's products is its Scoop System designed for hydraulic excavators. Using the Scoop System customers can increase productivity by up to 25 per cent as well as reduce their fuel consumption and other running costs.

The company now has more than 200 employees, three manufacturing sites in and around Blaydon and offices in Germany, China and Japan. More and more companies now specify the Miller Quick Coupler as standard, that wise choice being driven by the need to use the right-sized attachment every time and recognition that quality remains key in an ever competitive market.

At the start of the 21st century as pioneers of the pin pick-up hydraulic quick coupler system and with continual reinvestment, Miller (UK) Ltd and its management team confidently expect to maintain the Company's position as the market leader and aim to be the premier bucket and coupler manufacturer worldwide. This mission is well on the way to being achieved as the firm is the only pin pick-up manufacturer to supply the world's leading OEMs (Original Equipment Manufacturers), namely CAT, JCB, Hitachi, Komatsu, CNH and

Top left: *The famous Miller quick coupler under construction.* ***Above left:*** *The future looks bright, Miller 25 years on and their recently acquired facility affords ample opportunity for further expansion on an 18 acre site!* ***Right:*** *Keith Miller, Company Chairman.* ***Below:*** *Millers new corporate headquarters, Cramlington, Northumberland.*

From Tokyo to Tyneside

'Will we have to use chop sticks in the works canteen, like?' The last few decades have seen the people of North East become familiar with foreign companies investing in manufacturing facilities in the region. Almost imperceptibly Japanese companies in particular have helped to regenerate much of Tyneside's industry, building new factories and refurbishing old ones and bringing much needed employment and prosperity to the area after decades of industrial decline .

Of course it was all very mysterious to begin with. It wasn't just a case of worrying about chop sticks in the canteen; after all what food might be on offer - didn't the Japanese like raw fish? Would workers have to wear kimonos for work; would we have to bow to the bossses in polite Japanese fashion, and might the new employers expect their workers to learn the Japanese language and encourage them to take up flower arranging and paper folding?

Right: *An aerial view of the site in the early days.*
Below: *HRH Prince Charles officially opens the Komatsu plant in July 1987.*

The good news was jobs; the bad news might have been anything that the imagination could conjure up about that mysterious island nation of Japan, located on the far side of the world yet in many respects so similar to Britain.

And one aspect of the Japanese national character identical to that of the British was a belief in hard graft and enterprise. The Japanese had no particular wish to make workers from the North East learn their strange looking writing or eat sushi and rice, but they did admire their reputation in engineering and manufacturing skills enough to want to locate factories here.

In the early 1960s a small company involved in the heavy plant equipment market was number three in the then small Japanese market. Today's industrial giant Komatsu, named after the Japanese town where it has its origins, was founded in 1921 to make hydraulic excavators: in the opening years of the 1960s the company's management decided that the long term survival and prosperity of the company depended on their ability to match their biggest and best competitor in the world - at that time Caterpillar which had a 60 per cent share of the world market.

Thirty years later Komatsu would be making a quarter of the world's excavators and substantial profits - whilst the share of its chief competitor had slipped to just 30 per cent - and it was making a loss.

The key to Komatsu's triumph was not simply its managers' strategic vision but more importantly how that vision created a sense of purpose throughout the organisation. The focus of that vision was a simple statement of strategic intent: 'Beat Cat'. The goal for all Komatsu staff was extremely clear: beat Caterpillar in sales, service, product quality and parts whenever and wherever it was a competitor. And though the company could not have known it when its path to glory was formulated, following that path would eventually lead it to the North East of England.

During the early 1980s, as part of Komatsu Ltd's strategy to manufacture its products closer to the market, the United Kingdom was selected as the location for the company's fourth overseas manufacturing base. The UK was selected because of its enthusiasm for inward investment, and, with English the preferred language of Komatsu Ltd, communications were excellent.

Within England the North East was chosen in particular because of its long tradition of engineering skills and the availability of a skilled labour pool.

Komatsu UK was established in December 1985 with a share capital of £13 million and was a 100 per cent owned subsidiary of Komatsu Ltd. The share capital would subsequently be increased to more than £28 million, held equally between Komatsu Ltd and Komatsu Europe International NV.

The company took over the former Birtley premises of Caterpillar, its main rival, with the specific aim of producing machines for the European market.

Top left: *The Assembly line under construction.* ***Above right and right:*** *Two views of the factory during and after construction.*

During 1986, with just 60 staff, the facility underwent substantial refurbishment in preparation for production to begin the following year. The company was greatly honoured when HRH the Prince of Wales officiated at the factory's opening ceremony on 16th July 1987.

A mix of British and Japanese work practices would produce some interesting results: not least that absenteeism would be just two per cent of the British average. Yet there was no traditional clocking on or off, nor any penalties for lateness. A cornerstone of success would be trust, ownership and responsibility. Komatsu workers would start their shifts with stretching exercises to get the blood circulating.

Above left and right: *Views of the main office during and after construction.* ***Below:*** *Workers at Komatsu starting work the Japanese way back in 1987.*

Komatsu UK soon became one of the premier excavator manufacturers in Europe, and in 1988, with a local parts content level of 60 per cent (later 80 per cent) the company was formally accepted as a European manufacturer by the EEC Commission.

The company would soon become involved in a number of on-going community projects. One such project is the Pinetree Centre. Founded in 1989 the Pinetree Centre occupies around half of Komatsu's office space. The office facility, made available for charitable work on a short term peppercorn rent, was founded by Komatsu UK, City action Trust, Gateshead MBC and Entrust Ltd. The charity provides training and assistance to physically handicapped and long-term unemployed people in the North of England.

marketing excavators in addition to manufacturing them. The Working Gear Division was established in 1998 for the supply of non-standard equipment, and a product demonstration area and viewing pavilion was created in addition to an established visitor centre. The change to a 'Business Unit' culture along with other market forces would see business grow from 1600 'units' being sold in 1996 to plans to produce double that figure annually by 2002.

Today Komatsu UK is leaving no stone unturned in its pursuit of furthering the business. The company's vision is no longer simply 'Beat the Cat' but to be market leader in Europe: if the history of the company to date is to be a guide that ambition will be achieved through the continual development of safe, reliable and innovative products and services which lead in turn to unparalleled customer satisfaction.

Over the last two decades Japanese names, Japanese customs and Japanese faces have become familiar on Tyneside - and, despite any early misconceptions about catering arrangements, all without exception have been welcomed. The Japanese who have come to live in the North East have discovered what we have known all along: that the folk on Tyneside are the friendliest and most welcoming in the whole of the United Kingdom. And in the process we've discovered that it really is possible to eat chips with chop sticks. No, only kidding; what we've really discovered is that the Japanese are pretty much like us, and that companies like Komatsu are just as keen to see

Above left: *Danish visitors at the Komatsu factory in January 1988.* ***Below:*** *A recent aerial view of the Komatsu factory.*

At employee level the KUK's Sports and Social Committee, supported by the company, has raised more than £80,000 through sponsored events; money raised has been donated to local charities selected by employees. More recently the company has established a Charity Panel, in addition to the sports and Social committee, to review and make donations on behalf of the company to the local community.

Whilst seeking to enhance the quality of life outside the factory gates the quality of life inside was not forgotten either: in 1990 a Japanese garden was officially opened by HRH the Princess Royal. More industrial investment was in progress too.

Further investment in 1990 and 1991 saw the establishment of Komatsu UK's Design and Test facilities. Following that substantial investment the company launched its first wheeled excavator in 1992, the PW 170-5. Since 1992 the company's product range has increased to include five KUK-designed wheeled excavators (13-22 tonne) and 13 crawler excavators (13 - 75 tonne). Since 1994 the company has designed and completed some nine excavator models.

By 1995 Komatsu UK had produced no fewer than 10,000 excavators in the North East and in the process gained the ISO 9001 award as well as the Queen's Award for Export. In 1994 the North East began exporting excavators to the USA - more intriguingly exports were even being made to Japan.

With more than 400 employees now on site production was steaming ahead: in 1993 turnover had reached £78 million, by 1996 output had passed £110 million.

In 1996 the responsibilities of Komatsu UK changed with the formation of 'The Hydraulic Excavator Business Unit'. At this point the UK company became responsible for

Mmmm! Just smell that coffee

According to the old saying there's an awful lot of coffee in Brazil. But there's also a heck of a lot of coffee in Newcastle: a great deal of it produced by the celebrated firm of Pumphreys.

Unlike money, coffee really does grow on trees, or to be more precise bushes. And for those who thought its natural form was a brown powder there's a lot more to coffee production than simply putting it in jars.

Coffee is a drink made from the roasted and ground seeds or berries from any of several species of the coffee shrub; a plant which today is cultivated in the tropics all across the globe. And what gives coffee its unique kick is the large amount of the stimulant caffeine which it contains.

Above: *George Richardson Pumphrey (left) and his brother Thomas.* ***Right:*** *An invoice dated 1858.* ***Below:*** *The Old Flesh Market, 1827.*

But coffee has not always been as popular as it is today: indeed in the distant past it was quite unknown, not just in Europe but everywhere. Coffee drinking actually began in Arab countries in the 14th century where the coffee plant grows wild and where alcohol is forbidden to the followers of Islam.

The drink was not introduced to Europe until the Arabs had been enjoying the pleasures of unsweetened, bitter, black coffee for three centuries or more. The first coffee-houses opened in London in the 17th century, offering coffee which was by now being sweetened with sugar and served white with milk or cream - an innovation first tried by Italian Capuchin monks - from where we get our word 'cappucino'.

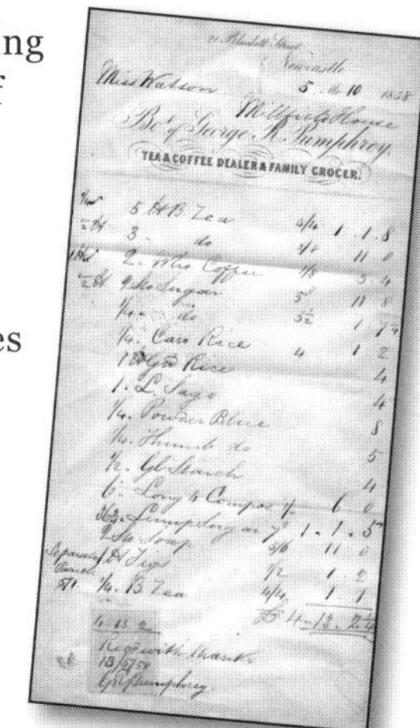

Miss Watson 5 . 10 1858

Bot of George R. Pumphrey

TEA & COFFEE DEALER & FAMILY GROCER.

Though an expensive drink coffee was a popular alternative to alcohol amongst those who could afford it and wanted to get some work done. Coffee-houses would thrive, and in the process become such important meeting places for businessmen that institutions such as the stock market and Lloyd's would trace their origins to such venues.

Meanwhile coffee production was increased commercially to meet increasing demand. The wild coffee shrub grows to around 17 ft tall. For commercial purposes it is pruned down to around 7 ft and is fully fruit-bearing in five or six years and keeps producing a crop for 30 years or more. The coffee shrub grows best on frost free hillsides with moderate rainfall, and over the last four hundred years coffee plantations have been established all across the world far from the plant's native Arabia by keen entrepreneurs. The world's largest coffee producers today are Brazil, Colombia and the Ivory Coast.

But those three countries are just the main producers; many other countries too have thriving coffee plantations such as those in Kenya or in Jamaica's Blue Mountains, which, at least according to coffee connoisseur James '007' Bond, produces the best coffee in the world.

One place of course where it is definitely impossible to grow coffee is the North East of England. But if we can't grow it we certainly like to drink plenty of it. And the North East's favourite brand is Pumphreys.

Pumphreys of Newcastle has a history which can be traced back to the year 1750.

The business was established by one Leigh Smith in what was then the Flesh Market opposite the Bigg Market and was later sold to George Richardson in 1800. George Richardson is described in contemporary documents as a Quaker, a businessman, tanner, grocer and a dealer in tea.

George Richardson was succeeded by his son

This page: *Early interior and exterior photographs of Pumphrey & Carrick Watson Ltd.*

Henry Richardson in 1835. Around the same time the street in which the firm had traded, and which had earlier been renamed Union, Street now became today's familiar Cloth Market.

Henry Richardson had two nephews Thomas Pumphrey and George Richardson Pumphrey. In 1853 George Richardson Pumphrey, then aged 23, bought a grocery business in Newcastle's Blackett Street taking his younger brother Thomas, then aged 21, as his shop assistant.

The following year however Thomas Pumphrey left his brother's shop to go and join his uncle Henry Richardson in the Cloth Market which was by then trading as Henry Richardson & Co. Thomas took over the business when his uncle retired in 1858.

George Richardson Pumphrey ran his business in Blackett Street until his tragically early death at the age of just 32 in 1862. As a result of his older brother's death Thomas Pumphrey now formed a partnership with his friend T Carrick Watson. Watson would run the Blackett Street business as Pumphrey & Watson for seven years until 1869 when he became the sole proprietor, leaving Thomas to concentrate on the business in Cloth Market.

By the time he was 39 in 1870 Thomas Pumphrey's business was thriving sufficiently for him to completely rebuild the premises in Cloth Market: T Carrick Watson would entirely rebuild his premises in Blackett Street in 1887.

By 1911 the business in Cloth Market had become T Pumphrey & Son and the Blackett Street business had become T Carrick Watson & Son. But the 50 year friendship between the two proprietors had persisted and on St Valentine's day 1911 the two businesses merged to form a new company: Pumphrey & Carrick Watson Ltd.

Sadly just two months after the merger Thomas Pumphrey, by now aged 78, died at his home 6 Summerhill Grove in Newcastle.

Despite Thomas Pumphrey's death his business continued to thrive and 'Pumphrey's Coffee' would become a household name throughout the North East.

Business was however seriously disrupted by the outbreak of war - both in 1914 and in 1939 when merchant shipping was seriously disrupted. For four years between 1914 and 1918, and for six years between 1939 and 1945, many folk almost forgot what coffee tasted like. Some caffeine addicts were even reduced to trying to make their own 'coffee' by roasting acorns. Others, more lucky, managed to get hold of what was now a rare commodity through contacts with American forces based in Britain.

Above: *Company letterheads from 1938 (top) and 1953.* ***Right:*** *Malcolm Archer serving with his mother Mrs D Archer in their shop in Newcastle Grainger Market, 1968.*

After the second world war however the grocery trade began to flounder and it became necessary to close the Blackett Street branch: the business in the Cloth Market though, with its very busy roasting department, and coffee rooms above, continued to flourish.

Indeed after the war coffee sales began a steady increase, and tea drinking began a slow but steady decline: a trend that continues to this day. Why should that be so? Some might point to price and say that in relative terms the cost of coffee has come down: others would point to fashion and the ongoing desire to emulate everything American - after all, Hollywood stars never seemed to drink tea, they always drank coffee, and who wouldn't want to be more like them?

But meanwhile the grocery side of Pumphreys continued its decline, and in 1974 the decision was taken to close that aspect of operations and to move the coffee business into the Old George Yard behind the shop, and to continue supplying the catering trade from there. The move would allow the main building, which was in great demand for use as a public bar, to be sold and so kick start what would become the Bigg Market party area - though the sale of the property would not be complete until 1977.

By 1983 Pumphreys had been in the Cloth Market for 230 years, but that was to change. That year the business, now Pumphreys Coffee Ltd, was bought by Mr CJ Archer who moved the enterprise to Blaydon on Tyne, home of the Blaydon Races.

At Bridge Street, Blaydon on Tyne a new 40,000 sq ft factory provided warehousing and roasting facilities. Customers now included hotel groups, restaurant chains, local authorities, coffee shops, tea rooms and offices all over the country.

Though much at Pumphreys may be new its old values are still shared by the present directors Stuart and Malcolm Archer. They are both proud to be able offer to the catering trade and the public a choice of over 80 different coffees or teas, all freshly prepared with the traditional Pumphreys' care.

A popular addition to the Pumphreys' range is coffee sourced from Capeuleu, a company which specialises in growing coffee organically in its own plantation in Guatemala, an ecological haven where the plants are carefully nurtured in the complete absence of artificial chemicals.

Those who visit the Pumphreys' roasting rooms and factory shop in Bridge Street today, and see for themselves the care and attention given to the production of coffee, will soon find, as have generations before them, that 'There's no Coffee like Pumphreys' Coffee'.

***Top left:** Mr Malcolm Archer in discussions with the Plantation Manager at Capeuleu an organic coffee farm in Antigua, Guatemala. **Above left:** Some ripe coffee cherries. **Below:** A staff photograph, 2003.*

Mirror, mirror ...

Break a mirror and it's seven years bad luck. But what if you make one? Does that give you seven years of good luck? A company which should know is Chameleon Mirrors.

The key figure behind Chameleon Mirrors, Philip Fieldsend, came to Newcastle in September 1973 to take a BSc degree at Newcastle Polytechnic in General Practice Surveying; his aim was to become an agricultural auctioneer and valuer.

During his course Philip undertook two sabbatical years: one as Social Secretary and one as Treasurer of the Students Union.

In 1975 during the celebrations for Her Majesty's Silver Jubilee, Philip became involved in the organising of the Jesmond Festival in an area of the city. Taking the opportunity of running a stall in Jesmond's Acorn Road Philip had nothing to sell, but a fellow student introduced him to a line in Elvis, John Travolta and Coca-Cola decorative mirrors.

The entire stock was sold out by lunch-time and had to be quickly replenished. It was a memorable introduction to the world of commerce.

Although Philip went on to finish his degree, and achieve the qualification necessary to take up a career in auctions and valuations, the world of Chartered Surveying proved far less alluring than selling decorative mirrors every day with its instant financial rewards.

Market trading in the 1970s provided a good living. The Quayside Sunday Market was the only retail venue in the North East able to operate on a Sunday and naturally stall space was at a premium. Obtaining a stall on the Quayside offered Philip the chance to create the foundations of a good business specialising in selling decorative 'pub' mirrors, a speciality which would remain the backbone of the business to this day.

But many other commercial paths would be taken over the intervening years.

After leaving Newcastle Polytechnic in 1978 Philip's first business base was a back street double garage behind Jesmond Road, just off the city centre. Two years later shop premises in Manor House Road, Jesmond were taken with storage in the basement. The shop was known as Cloud Nine; it sold ceramic novelties such as cups with feet, flamingo soup-tureens, cow-shaped butter dishes and storage jars shaped like terraced houses. Pub mirrors were however sold only through the market trading side of the business.

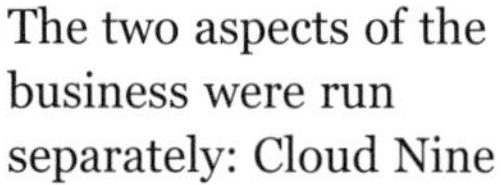

The two aspects of the business were run separately: Cloud Nine

Right and above right: *Chameleon's premises in the 1980s at 60 Bond Hanover Street.*

was run by Julie Green. Joining forces with Helen Morris and Michael Chippendale the Cloud Nine name was later changed to Shabbytat. The new name was a play on words - an obvious dig at the far larger Habitat, but Shabbytat was a registered limited company and no-one could take the trading name away from its owners.

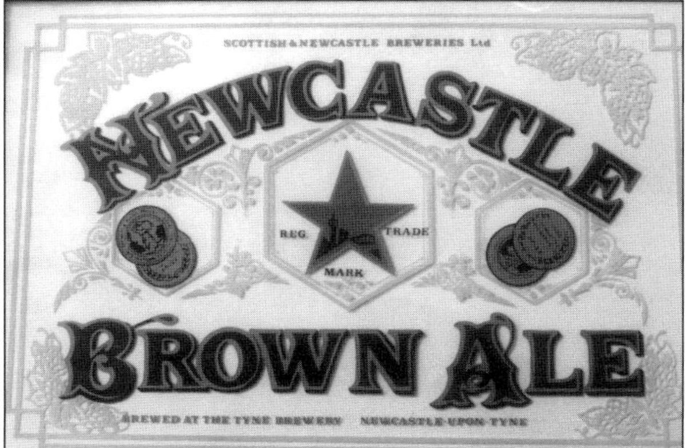

Shabbytat had two slogans; as its name suggest that is what it sold: Faults, Flaws and Foul Ups - Trash, Trinkets and Trivia. Four years later as the fad for funky ceramics passed, rents in the city centre increased and the core mirror business increased the retail side was closed. Philip still harbours hopes of one day reincarnating those happy days at Shabbytat.

Meanwhile however the tiny firm was still trading in 'pub' mirrors and had moved that operation on from lock ups and the cellar in Manor House Road to premises along the bank of the river, at the Close. Former bonded warehousing at 60 Bond Hanover Street now became the new base.

The premises were not however particularly suitable for warehousing mirrors: in most parts the ceiling were just 1.85m - perfect for storing pallets of spirits and wine. At least it was large having 8,300 sq metres, though spread out over seven floors and with no lifts.

In fact the firm occupied only three floors, but at least it would be possible to expand. Julie Green, Heather Matthews, Michael Chippendale and Philip Fieldsend now formed a new company, Chameleon Ltd, in 1983.

When the business had started selling pub mirrors in 1978 there had been 13 companies in the United Kingdom

Top: *The Shabbytat Store.* ***Above:*** *One of Chameleon's mirrors, with a local connection.*

producing that type of mirror. Chameleon bought its mirrors from seven of those companies, but as the craze subsided over the following decade so too did the number of manufacturers. Chameleon experienced a problem of supply so Philip and his partners bought in the frames separately from the mirrors and began to assemble them themselves.

Almost inevitably Chameleon now also soon began to experience difficulties in getting the right qualities of images and designs, so Chameleon now began printing on glass and had the silvering done by a company in Sunderland.

Over a five year period Chameleon gradually put the full manufacturing process together. By 1985 the firm was in complete control of printing on glass, making the frames and silvering the printed glass to give the mirrors their reflective surface. All the work was being done at Hanover Street even though the premises were far from being suitable for manufacturing.

Printing on glass now led to printing of different kinds of material. A 'carousel' was acquired which allowed printing to be done on T-shirts. Chameleon now started its own mail order service for its Alternative sportswear which was advertised in many magazines. Chameleon also obtained a contract from Viz comics to print its comic characters such as Sid the Sexist, Johnny Fartpants and Biffa Bacon on to T-shirts for Viz's own mail order sales. By now Chameleon had become known for printing on to clothing and had started to print a wider range of clothing items for the workplace and for schools.

Chameleon was growing. The two original people still involved in the company by 1988 were Philip Fieldsend and Heather Matthews; now they began looking for new accommodation. All the premises along the banks of the Tyne were becoming attractive for residential development and Chameleon's long-unsuitable premises were now sold for housing, enabling a more suitable manufacturing site to be bought with the proceeds of the sale.

The company now moved into the 4,000 sq metre former Osram light bulb factory at Dukesway in the Team Valley Trading Estate in Gateshead.

The move of all equipment, goods, material and personnel took four days and cost one week's lost production: but the pleasure of working in modern premises was unbelievable. Now Chameleon really began to expand. By 1989 the

Below: *Newcastle's Quayside Sunday Market.*

company was one of just two companies in the whole country which still made pub mirrors. The demand from wholesalers, retailers and the promotions industry took off in an extraordinary way. And not just from Britain: some 85 per cent of everything made was exported propelling Chameleon into the world of export awards and public prominence.

By 1990 annual turnover had grown to be worth a million pounds, though all would not be plain sailing yet. The increase in sterling's value in the mid 1990s caused a major headache for all companies reliant upon exports. Chameleon now began to be less competitive in world markets and began to look towards the home market once more, a market which had been largely neglected for eight years whilst the export market had been developed.

Top: *From left to right; Philip Fieldsend, Clive James, Heather Matthews and Ernie Wise at the presentation of the firm's first Export Achievement Award in 1989.* ***Below:*** *Some of the firm's directors and staff outside their premises.*

At the Team Valley factory Chameleon opened a small showroom in 1994 which attracted many new clients from the North of England. Revamping the production layout in 1999 provided the opportunity to increase the size of the showroom almost twenty-fold and create a complete wholesale and retail sales area.

Today Chameleon's customers include a wide cross-section of clients, though with the bulk of business still the supply of bulk orders for mirrors and pictures to retail outlets such as John Lewis. Promotional mirrors are manufactured under licence for the likes of Guinness, Jack Daniels, Coca Cola, Budweiser and Carlsberg. Elsewhere other developments include contract work on glass and mirrors for builders, show houses, and apartments, commercial premises, offices and gymnasia.

Today what has become Chameleon Design Ltd is a world player in its field and produces a wide range of quality, framed, bevelled mirrors, a spectrum of framed images, mostly with hand cut mounts, and a beautiful, complementary line of photo frames and chalk boards. Keeping a very close eye on trends and fashion, Chameleon has invested in some of its own publications as well as working very closely with American and European publishers; such attention to detail continues to ensure that Chameleon Ltd, like its namesake, is always changing, whilst at the same time continuing to offer both exclusive and licensed designs on high quality products at competitive prices.

Top marks for markets

Though there are many market towns there aren't many market cities: but the city of Newcastle has certainly earned that accolade.

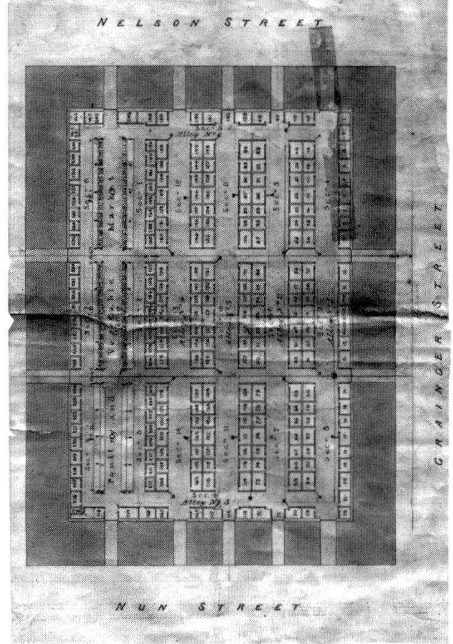

The modern Green Market for example, opened in 1976 as the successor to the older street market, was built by the City Council at a cost of more than £1 million. Today it forms part of the prestigious Eldon Square Shopping Centre. The Green Market offers fruit and vegetables and a separate fish market, in addition to other 'shopportunities' ranging from clothing repairs to an art gallery.

And today's Quayside Sunday Market is the now-legalised successor to a market which has been in existence since at least 1736

Newcastle's oldest market however is the open-air Bigg Market, which takes its name from 'bigg' a kind of barley once grown locally.

Marks and Spencer was started in Leeds' Kirkgate Market in 1884 by Michael Marks and Thomas Spencer. Famously Marks, a Jewish refugee from Russia, borrowed £5 and hired a small open-air market stall selling high quality goods at affordable prices; his trading motto was revolutionary: 'Don't ask the price, it's a penny'.

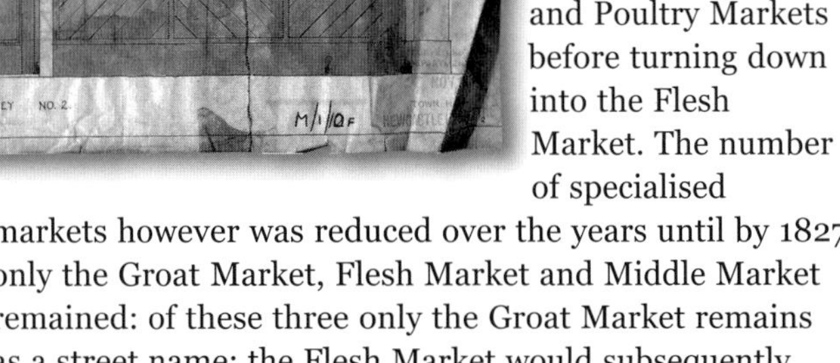

Of course Leeds may have been fine to begin with, but the real place to be was Newcastle. Hence, today, Newcastle's Grainger Market is home to the world's oldest Marks and Spencer store - the 'Marks and Spencer Original Penny Bazaar'. The Grainger Market branch opened in 1895 and has changed little over the years, having retained its original frontage: even the light fittings are original, though they have been converted from gas to electricity.

But, when they came to Newcastle's' famous Grainger Market at the end of the 19th century, Marks and Spencer were definitely the new kids on the block.

When King John made Newcastle upon Tyne a borough in 1216 there were already markets thriving in the area. For the most part those markets were strung out along the Great North Road, the already-ancient highway, which 700 years later would become the A1, and which was then the town's main thoroughfare.

By the 18th century the road entered the town by the Tyne Bridge near the site of today's Swing Bridge. Almost immediately the traveller came upon the Herb Market which had been there since 1723, and beyond that was the Fish Market opposite the Guildhall. Beyond those two markets the road swung around the hill of the Castle Keep, this part of the road being called The Side, before turning northwards past the church of St Nicholas (later becoming a cathedral) into the main market area which was divided by rows of buildings. The Iron Market lay opposite Amen Corner; continuing up the left hand side of the road one arrived at the Grot (Groat) Market with the Wool Market coming off it halfway up towards Middle Street. Turning back down the far side of the market one passed the Butter and Poultry Markets before turning down into the Flesh Market. The number of specialised markets however was reduced over the years until by 1827 only the Groat Market, Flesh Market and Middle Market remained: of these three only the Groat Market remains as a street name: the Flesh Market would subsequently

Above: *Early plans and elevations for Newcastle's Grainger Market.*

become known as the Cloth Market, another echo of the past which still features in the modern street map alongside Haymarket, Bigg Market and the Milk Market.

The end of the 18th century and the beginning of the 19th century brought to Newcastle a mushrooming growth which spread way beyond its still almost complete medieval walls. The impetus imparted by the industrial revolution and, in particular, the dawning of the railway age, was fast turning the town into a regional capital, whilst still retaining a largely medieval street plan.

Fortunately Newcastle contained a group of men who were to mastermind the rebuilding of much of the town centre in the very best Georgian style: builder and entrepreneur Richard Grainger, John Dobson, a visionary architect, and John Clayton the Town Clerk.

Richard Grainger was born into a poor background on Low Friar Street in 1797, the second son of a Quayside porter.

John Clayton was a close friend of Grainger's and was the son of the previous Town Clerk, Nathaniel Clayton.

The eldest of the trio, Architect John Dobson, was born in North Shields in 1787. He was apprenticed at the office of David Stephenson before going to London in 1809 to further his career before returning to Tyneside a year later.

The idea of town centre covered markets was as fashionable in the early 19th century as the fashion for out of town super stores

Above: *An artist's impression of Grainger Market in Victorian times.* ***Below:*** *A 19th Century aerial view of the Grainger Market and surroundings.*

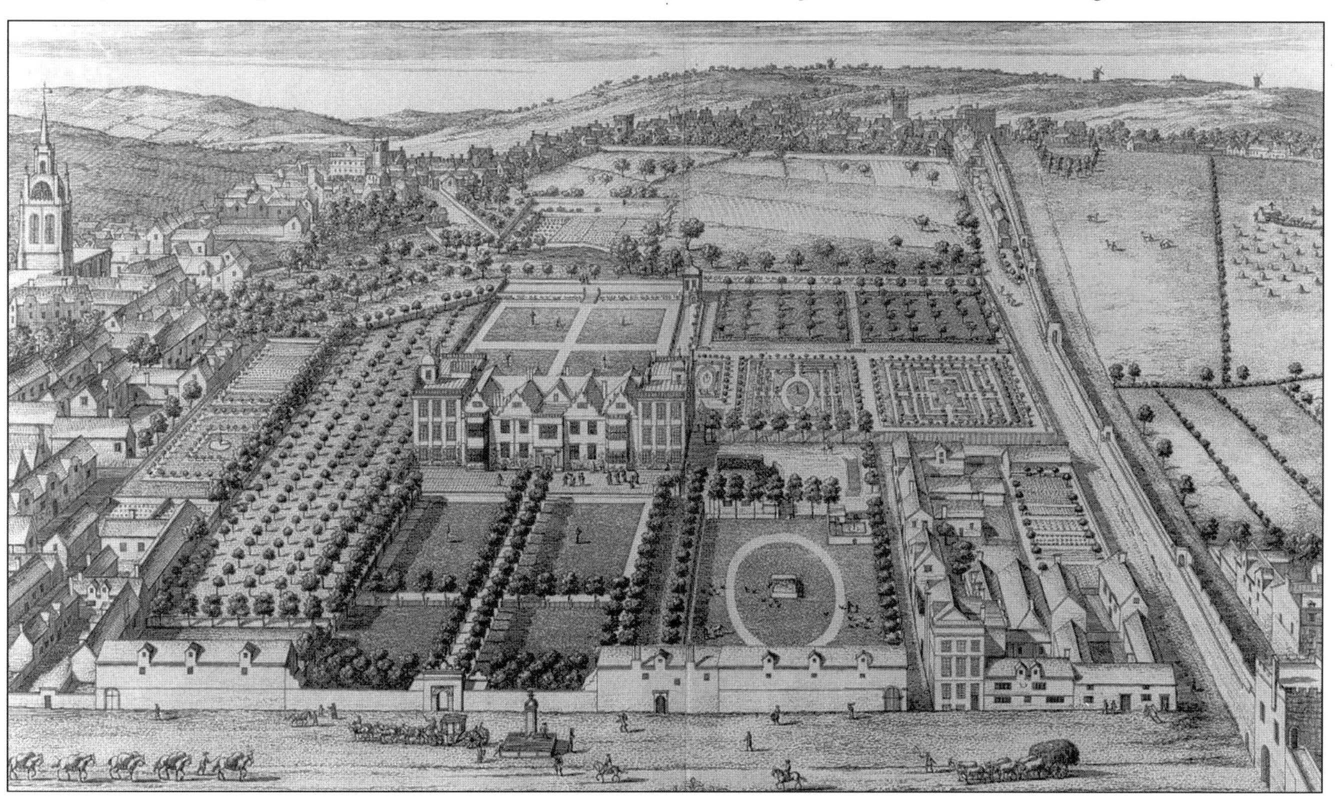

would become in the late 20th. Many towns and cities across England began to build new market halls, competing with one another to produce the most magnificent. Today many survive, though sadly most have been destroyed, either by the Luftwaffe during the course of the second world war or by thoughtless developers in the 1960s. Probably the best surviving example today is in the heart of Newcastle.

Carrying out Messrs Grainger, Dobson and Clayton's plans for a covered market for Newcastle required the demolition of the old Flesh Market which by this time had changed its name back to the Cloth Market and had occupied the site for 30 years. Richard Grainger acquired the site of the Nuns Field for £15,000. This was formerly a Benedictine Nunnery but was demolished by Robert Anderson in the 16th Century to dislodge squatters.

The Nuns Field, later Anderson Place, the residence of Sir John Anderson, and covering the area between Pilgrim Street and St Andrew's church in Newgate Street was also bought and the plans for redevelopment were able to proceed.

Before the two new markets were opened the sale of meat and vegetables was largely carried out on the streets, no doubt at great inconvenience for local residents and for those trying to pass along the narrow streets - and certainly far from being hygienic.

The Grainger Markets between Newgate Street and Grainger Street which, at the time they were built, were rightly considered to be the most spacious and magnificent in Europe. There was originally both a Flesh Market and a Vegetable Market on the same site, the latter being located in what would subsequently become the Grainger Arcade.

The markets were opened to the public on Saturday 24th October 1835, following a public dinner held in the Vegetable Market two days earlier attended by more than 2,000 individuals. On the day of the opening 'The bells rang out to many a merry peal, and the occasion was regarded by everyone as auspicious for the town'. The Vegetable Market was timber roofed with a huge cathedral like span of almost 60 feet in width

This page: *Early and mid twentieth century photographs inside Grainger Market.*

and some 314 feet in length. Unfortunately that magnificent roof was destined to be destroyed by fire: it was rebuilt in its present impressive steel girder fashion, and reopened to the public on 28th November 1901.

The remainder of the Market however is very much as it was when it opened before Queen Victoria's long reign began, apart that is from the obvious changes that electric lighting and new facades and shop fittings have brought about.

A remaining original feature of the market is the Weigh House. This was used by stall holders and buyers alike to check the weight of their purchases, and was once a legal requirement for all markets to have. Though the law may no longer require such a facility the weigh house has been retained and is now used by up to 700 people a day to check their own weight.

The Market is an historic building, preserved for posterity: but it is not a museum rather it is a vibrant, animated shopping place where the personal and individual service of the small shop is allied to prices that cannot be equalled. Today its stalls offer a range of goods far beyond the original conception of only meat and vegetables.

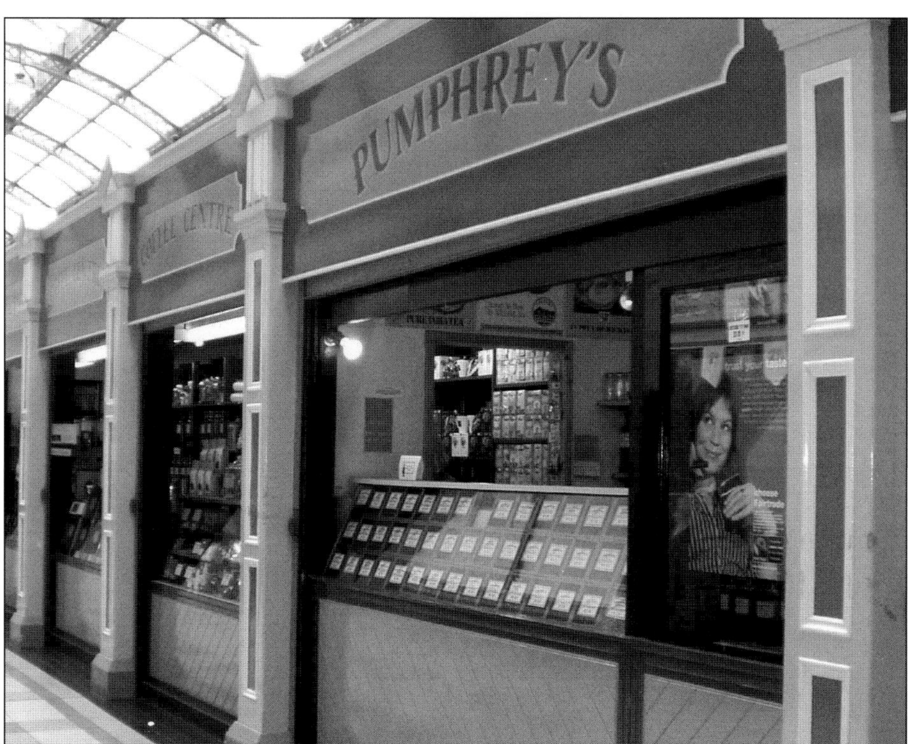

Now a Grade I listed building the market houses over 100 shops and stalls with a lettable area of some 38,000 square feet, making it still one of the largest market halls in the country. Fresh produce outlets make up the majority of stalls, many of which have been occupied by the same families for more than a century.

Markets certainly are at the heart of Newcastle, a town which, since its elevation in civic status in 1882, has surely merited the title of Britain's first market city.

Top right: *Commemorating Grainger Market Bicentenary.*
Above left: *One of the stalls in today's Grainger Market.*
Left: *Pumphreys Coffee shop.*

Start spreading the news

So what does the word 'Primula' mean to you? Yes, of course it's the name of a flower, but it's also the name of Britain's best-loved cheese spread, a product familiar to generations of housewives putting up sandwiches for hungry husbands and children, and it's the 'secret ingredient' of a thousand savoury recipes.

But where does Primula cheese spread come from - and how do they get it into tubes? Even we can't answer that last question, but we do know where it comes from - Kavli Ltd in Gateshead: but before that it came from Norway.

Olav Kavli was born in 1872 and grew up together with six brothers and sisters on a small west Norwegian farm near the port of Molde. The smallholding was quite humble; as a result Olav learnt at an early age that hard work was necessary to make ends meet. He often went down to the steamer pier in Molde and found inspiration watching the big ships which sailed from there. Becoming an international merchant of some kind was soon his dream.

By the age of 18 Olav had saved enough to invest in a steamer ticket to the town of Bergen, where he could gain some more work experience and start studying.

In 1893, by which time he was 21, Olav had obtained a licence as a self-employed merchant and started his own cheese-selling business.

Olav Kavli soon became a knowledgeable merchant and a good salesman. He

Above: *An advertising hoarding in the mid 1950s.*
Below: *A convoy of Kavli delivery lorries pictured in Piccadilly Square, London in the 1950s.*

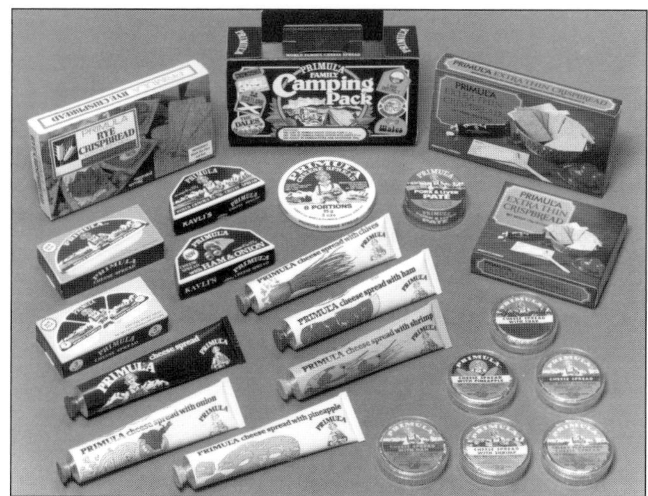

quickly expanded his range of cheeses. The business prospered and expanded across Norway. After several years of building a solid Norwegian business Olav turned his attention abroad.

Packing a suitcase with cheese, Olav travelled to Britain, Sweden and Denmark developing valuable trading contacts.

Once back in Norway, Olav now began to consider making his own cheese rather than selling other people's produce. That business would demand more space, and Olav acquired his own dairy in 1914.

Top: *Kavli's purpose built factory on the Team Valley industrial estate, shortly after it was built in 1961.*
Above: *A selection of Primula products from the 1970s.*
Right: *Kavli's Primula Girl with cheese box.*

It was on one of his many trips that Olav had the idea for a long-life spreadable cheese. In 1924 after countless unsuccessful attempts, sustained by hard work and undaunted faith in himself, he was finally able to unveil Primula - the world's first spreadable cheese.

But Olav wanted to present his cheese to customers in a distinctive way, something which would be seen by the general public as new and attractive, whilst also being functional. The result was a wooden box, shaped like a half-moon, with a girl holding a bunch of primulas (the first flowers of spring) on the label. Perhaps when choosing the Primula name Olav had in mind that his new product, like the flower, would be the first of many Kavli products to bloom in the coming years; if so, he was right.

The now famous and universally recognised Primula girl is a dairy maid wearing national Norwegian costume against a backdrop of Scandinavian mountains. Through the years she has always retained her basic features, though she has been allowed to change slightly with changing fashions.

Knut Kavli, Olav's son, joined his father as an equal partner in 1924, the same year that Primula cheese made its first appearance. Knut took on responsibility for the Norwegian end of the business while Kavli senior travelled the world and promoted Norway's newest export.

Knut had received advantages that Olav had never had. He was well

educated, with experience from foreign study trips and dairy operations, as well as a specialist knowledge of chemistry and physics.

Unlike his famous namesake, England's King Canute, Knut Kavli had an instinctive grasp of what was possible and now set out to achieve it. With his training and education Knut had a solid basis for turning his father's dreams into reality and driving the company forward. It was he who introduced the first cheese in a tube in 1929. Collapsible metal tubes had been in use for at least sixty years already; they had been invented by an Englishman who had developed them for holding oil paint for artists. The first known food substance to be put in them was mustard, and by the close of the 19th century they had recently become familiar in many homes as containers for toothpaste. It was to fall to Knut Kavli to realise that tubes which could be used for mustard and toothpaste could just as easily be used to contain the Kavli company's spreadable cheese. The concept would remain a cornerstone of the business into the 21st century, by which time a whole range of Kavli cheese products would be available in tubes.

Knut also successfully established factories in Sweden and Austria, and was able to create new cheese variants for each country, based on the variations in raw materials and milk available in each location. Even before the second world war, Primula was being sold in more than 50 countries world-wide.
In 1936, as war loomed in Europe, Kavli Ltd relocated its

Top: *The Team Valley industrial estate looking busier in the late 1960s.* ***Above right:*** *Primula's range of products pictured in the 1980s.*

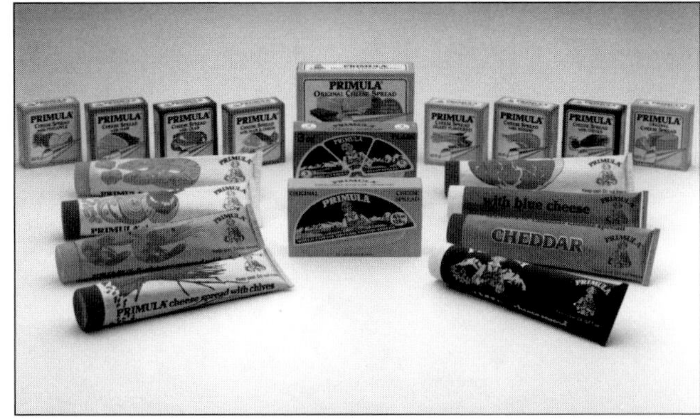

Austrian factory to England. A factory was established in Cramlington, outside Newcastle, but after a few years, the business expanded and it moved to a brand new, and much bigger, factory located in the Team Valley near Gateshead. The move out of Austria proved to be a wise one. The subsequent German occupation of Norway would only serve to underline Knut Kavli's foresight. Happily for Briton's Primula cheese spread would still sustain them during the darkest days of the second world war, when Britain stood alone against the might of Hitler's armies.

By 1961 another new factory was needed, and construction began on the current site as one of the first businesses to move onto the Team Valley trading estate, the first purpose built industrial estate in Britain. Since then the 'new' factory has been enlarged and modernised several times over the years to keep pace with advances in customer requirements and in food manufacturing practice.

Today the Gateshead site employs around 110 people and produces in excess of 3,500 tonnes of Primula products each year.

As tastes and lifestyles have changed, so Primula has moved with the times and the brand was expanded in 1995 to include a range of high quality Primula Dips.

In 1997 Kavli acquired Castle MacLellan Foods, a specialist paté company based in Kircudbright, Scotland. Kalvi would successfully grow that business as a quality supplier to the major UK retailers.

2000 saw a major change to the classic Primula cheese-in-a-tube as the old metal tubes were replaced by modern plastic packaging, a first for this kind of product, and a change which resulted in significant sales growth.

More recently, with the successful launch in 2003 of Cheese Snacks for children, under a Scooby Doo character license, and Low Fat products, under the Weight Watchers brand, Kavli Ltd has extended its product range still further.

Today the Kavli Group operates factories in Norway and Sweden as well as in the UK, with sales operations in each of those countries in addition to Denmark and Finland. These sales operations are characterised by strong local knowledge and involvement, backed up by the resources of the larger group.

Trading policies and customs and practices are still based on the firm foundations of Olav and Knut's business ethics, a set of beliefs which are reflected in the humanitarian work supported by the Group's owner, the Kavli Foundation.

Knut Kavli, like his father before him, was a man with a strong social conscience. He had no family of his own, but he wanted to ensure that his company had a long-term and socially-engaged owner to carry on his work. So in 1962 Knut established a charitable foundation. The Kavli Foundation would become the sole shareholder and owner of the business. Through the Kavli Foundation, the Group is ensured stable ownership, while at the same time the Foundation's Articles of Association act as a guarantee that the Group gives back to society more than just taxes and customs duties.

A substantial amount of money is awarded each year to various humanitarian, cultural and research projects which are selected by the Kavli Foundation's Board - completely independently of the Group's commercial operations. Many good causes have been supported: in 2001, the Kavli Foundation entered into a long-term co-operation agreement with the Salvation Army, supporting world-wide humanitarian projects for the underprivileged. In 2001 and 2002, there were 15 projects in 6 different countries being supported by the Kalvi Foundation.

Above: *The Primula Cheese range today.*
Below: *Kavli's Team Valley base in 2003.*

One hundred years of quality

In 2003 Newcastle- based electrical company AE Fletcher (Electricals) Ltd (formerly Fletcher Bros.) celebrated its centenary. Today the business is one of the oldest and most respected electrical contractors in the North East of England having been involved in many prestigious jobs such as the floodlighting at St James' park as well as work on Australia House on the Swan House Roundabout and Stafford Shopping Mall.

Now based at Camperdown Industrial Estate, Killingworth the business is still family owned and managed, with a turnover of £5 million and rising. The firm's reputation has been built on extremely high standards of installation, customer care and flexible working practices with around 85 per cent of turnover coming from repeat business. Fletcher Electricals has been involved in many prestigious projects over its long history and can comfortably deal with contracts of up to £1.5 million.

No. 560.

The Electrical Contractors' Association (Incorporated).

(INCORPORATED 1904)

CERTIFICATE OF MEMBERSHIP.

This is to Certify that Walter Fletcher (Fletcher Bros) of 73 High Friar Street, Newcastle-on-Tyne was admitted a Member of The Electrical Contractors' Association (Incorporated), on the Twenty second day of December 1909.

Given under the Common Seal of the Electrical Contractors' Association (Incorporated), at London this 22nd day of December 1909.

Secretary. President.

The firm was founded in 1903 by Walter and Louis Fletcher working from premises in Newcastle's High Friar Street before subsequently moving the business to Blackett Street.

It was a brave, even inspired, move to set up an electrical contracting business in the very early years of the 20th century. Queen Victoria had died only two years previously. The jury

***Above:** The firm's Certificate of Membership of The Electrical Contractors Association, dated 22nd December, 1909. **Below:** Louis and Walter Fletcher at an Electrical Contractors Association Dinner in 1909.*

was still out on whether this new fangled electricity stuff was really the wave of the future or just a fad which would suddenly disappear. And besides, apart from powering trams, what could you use it for?

Probably the most obvious use was for lighting. Many folk would still be using gaslights in their homes in the 1950s but even so in 1903 the most obvious application of electricity in people's homes was for light. The incandescent filament lamp had been demonstrated in the United Kingdom by Joseph Swan in 1878 and in the USA in the following year by Thomas Edison. Now a market was beginning to emerge amongst the better off to have electricity installed in their homes, even if the number of other domestic uses: the electric iron, the electric cooker and the electric fire were probably the few other uses to which the new source of power could be conveniently used - but they were certainly significantly more expensive than the coal and gas alternatives. So why bother?

Few people back then would have predicted the total dominance which electricity would exert over all our lives a century hence. But still there was enough interest to make venturing into the new trade attractive to two enterprising young men who knew enough to be able to explain to a suspicious public that electricity wouldn't leak out if a plug was removed from a socket.

In the beginning the firm had no vans or cars. All the gear was carried by hand or, if it was a large contract, a hand cart was hired for town centre jobs. For out of town work the gear was delivered to the site by wholesalers such as Gledson's on Blackett Street near Fletcher's own base at number 63, and five decades later the firm still trade with Gledson's under the guise of Newey and Eyre.

At first electrical work was mostly carried out by joiners using wood to cap and case the cables: aesthetics were more important than the integrity of the electrical installation. Direct current was still in use and all the cables, sockets and switches were around twice the size of what they are today.

In Edwardian England few people knew much about electricity. Domestic electricity was only for the rich, with most fixtures and fittings being made of brass with expensive glass chandeliers. Cable was lead sheathed, something which needed careful handling to avoid kinks.

Candles needed to be used for all loft and under-floor work: stories of apprentices getting trapped under floor boards were common as older electricians screwed down floor boards as a prank - many young lads were lost for hours.

But despite such hardships lots of lads still wanted to become electricians, after all electricians wore shirt, collars and ties for their job, even if they did carry boiler suits in bags. Tradesmen had a high standing in society and were well regarded for their skills. As a result an apprentice gave plenty of respect to the electrician training him. That training included carrying all the tools and pushing the barrow - even as far as the coast seven miles away!

Walter's two sons, Albert and Alfred, eventually joined the firm as apprentices themselves. The former served as a Warrant Officer, the highest rank a non-commissioned

Top left: *Alfred Fletcher, Walter's son.* ***Right:*** *Albert Fletcher, Walter's son, pictured on his wedding day to Marguerite in 1942.*

officer can attain, in the REME during the second world war, before returning to the business to become its proprietor and Managing Director: the latter, who had served as a leading seaman in the Royal Navy, acted as storeman, appliance repairer and scourge of apprentices whom he would dangle out of the second floor window if they proved troublesome.

In the early days of the company work was all in the city centre, but it gradually progressed further out using trolley buses, trains, buses and carriers.

Once on the job, not only was there frequently no electric light to illuminate dark corners, neither were there any electric drills to save muscle power. The holes for all fixings on walls, ceilings and concrete floors were done using a hammer and a Rawlplug tool - a narrow pointed chisel, since rendered all but obsolete by the ubiquitous electric hammer drill. Switchboards were built up on a metal frame with all the necessary drilling done using a brace and bit.

Amongst the many employees who would work for Fletcher's for more than 20 years and more was Bill Nixon In 1955, at 16 years old, Bill Nixon joined the business: he was paid less than a shilling per hour for a 48 hour week over 5 $^1/_2$ days per week: but despite the low wages he stayed for 48 years, eventually becoming site foreman!

Bill Nixon recalls that when working on pithead baths for the NCB all the wiring had to be fixed every nine inches with a clip and screw. After marking out the runs and the holes the foreman, Fred Bain, had all the hands ready with hammers and Rawlplug tools and set the men off hammering and singing in time until all the holes were drilled: Fred said it was his 'singalong production line'.

***Top right:** The firm's premises on Blackett Street, pictured in the late 1960s. **Left:** Joe Willis. **Above right:** Albert's son, Alistair, who took over the day to day running of the company from Joe Willis in 1975.*

They were happy days: all the electricians were football mad and would carry footballs around for a game at lunch break - unless of course it was raining in which case it would be that other ever-ready standby, a card school.

The company was a founder member of the North East branch of the ECA - the Electrical Contractors Association and the NICEIC - the National Inspection Council for Electrical Installation Contracting, as well as all employees being 100 per cent CSCS (Construction Skills Certification Scheme) accredited and an electro technical invigilating centre.

Fletcher Electricals sold electrical appliances and fittings in Blackett Street until the early 1970s when plans for Eldon Square were developed. From there the company moved to Ouse Street during a period which saw business expansion: with that expansion came an increasingly professional attitude. Management became more formal as the workload increased and jobs began to be taken far away from Newcastle.

A.E. FLETCHER
(ELECTRICALS) LIMITED

Despite its small beginnings today Fletcher Electricals now has dedicated staff for all areas of its business including estimation, engineering, autocad technicians, inspection, testing and health and safety. The company entered the computer age in 1984 investing an astonishing £18,000 in an estimating computer: the machine was however so complicated no-one dared use it. The firm had to wait several years more until Alistair Fletcher's son, Christian, was old enough to join the firm and build, install and manage an integrated computer system. Today the company uses the very latest computer software to help with estimates and design, and for many other aspects of its work.

ECA
1901
2001

This Certificate is issued by the Electrical Contractors' Association, in its Centenary Year to

A E Fletcher (Electricals) Ltd

in recognition of it being one of the 100 oldest full member companies of the Association, in grateful appreciation for its continued support since

1909

By the 21st century, and the company's centenary in 2003, AE Fletcher (Electricals) Ltd with a permanent staff of over 70, was providing electrical contracting and design maintenance services to many well known clients such as Marks & Spencer Plc (a client of Fletcher Electricals Ltd for over seven decades), ASDA Stores, NHS Trusts, Transco, AMEC, Midland Bank Plc, Halifax Plc, Kier Northern, all local universities, Sir John Fitzgerald Breweries and to numerous other organisations in the North East, Yorkshire and the Midlands.

The 19th century was rightly called the age of steam. Steam power was found everywhere: in ships, railway locomotives, powering factories, fairground rides and agricultural machinery. But if the 19th century was the steam age then the 20th would be the age of electricity: and the Fletcher brothers' business was in the right place at exactly the right time. Their success was also made possible, in no small part, by the loyalty and dedication given to the family by their staff, both past and present, to whom the latest generation of Fletchers will always be grateful.

The 20th century saw electrical power installed in every home, every factory and every office. Competitors like gas lights, flat irons and coal-fired stoves passed into history. Homes have become filled with radios, televisions and computers. And through all those decades of change the firm Walter and Louis Fletcher founded has been at the forefront of delivering exactly what the emerging modern world most needed.

Top left: *St James's Park where many an hour was spent by the football mad staff of Fletcher's.* ***Top right:*** *A company letterhead.* ***Left:*** *The certificate presented to A E (Electricals) Ltd in 2001, in recognition of the firm being one of the 100 oldest full member companies of the Electrical Contractors Association.* ***Below:*** *Staff pictured outside the company premises, 2003.*

Solid foundations

One of the greatest changes to the lives of Newcastle folk since the end of the second world war has been the improvement to our homes. Older folk, and many not so old, will recall streets of houses unfit for human habitation. And even the better homes lacked amenities we now take for granted: central heating, double glazing and instant hot water.

But even 'modern' houses built since the war ended in 1945 are no longer new, despite what some of us think. That's one reason why there is an increasingly strong demand for brand new homes, built to far higher specification than existed in the post war decades. And one of the best known local names in the housebuilding business is Bowey Homes.

The Bowey Group has been building, not only houses but also a solid reputation since the original firm was founded by the present Chairman's grandfather almost a century ago.

As one the largest family-owned construction groups in the North of England Bowey has been responsible for building many of the commercial and residential properties in the region including schools, hospitals, offices and family homes. The Group's commitment to embracing the best of both traditional and modern techniques and materials has ensured, and continues to ensure that only the highest quality results are achieved in every sector of the building industry.

The business was founded in 1907 by Ralph Bowey senior who was helped by just one or two employees in running his tiny firm.

At the time the fledgling enterprise was based in Byker, originally at a corner shop in Gordon Street, but by 1936 the firm had moved to Mason Street in Byker before moving yet again to Raby Street.

Little is known about the firm during the inter-war years, but clients included local authorities as well as local businesses such as Thomas Hedley, which would later become Proctor & Gamble. In addition to being a public works contractor Ralph Bowey also occasionally built houses.

***Top:** The firm's first premises on Gordon Street.*
***Top right:** Company founder, Ralph Bowey Snr.*
***Above right:** An early building project.*
***Right:** The firms joinery shop in the 1960s.*

Company founder, Ralph Bowey, died after the second world war and his business, now Ralph Bowey & Son Ltd, which had been largely dormant during the course of the war, was taken over by the founder's son, Ralph Bowey junior. Riding on a surge of post-war reconstruction and new economic confidence the company enjoyed decades of extraordinary growth and prosperity.

By the early 1950s the company had relocated once more. In 1953 the firm moved its base to offices on the Great North Road, opposite Hancock Museum, and also opened a depot at William Street, South Gosforth. New offices were built at William Street in the early 1960s.

The main growth since the 1950s was at South Gosforth where adjoining properties were acquired over the years, eventually totalling five acres, and which at its peak included 20,000 sq ft of office space, 25,000 sq ft of joinery workshops and 15,000 sq ft of engineering workshops in addition to assorted stores.

In 1953 joinery works had been built at William Street: the Gosforth Joinery Works Ltd was formed there as a subsidiary company: this was the first subsidiary of what would in future become the Bowey Group. Two years later the firm's painting and decorating activities were transferred to a second subsidiary, Gosforth Painters Ltd.

In 1960 the civil engineering firm of William T Wallace and Son Ltd was brought in to the Group orbit and with it came a first class reputation together with the newly acquired company's ability in civil engineering and tarmacadam work. The following year a new company - J Ward (Electrical) Ltd was formed to carry out all kinds of electrical installation. By 1964 the company also had a seven acre plant depot near Earsdon.

A keynote of progress in those years would be stepping up mechanisation: by 1964, in hastening that trend, the company had built up one of the most comprehensive

***Top:** The post-war housing boom.* ***Above left:** Adding drainage lines for the Shulton premises at Seaton Delaval in the late 1950s.* ***Above right:** The founder's son, Ralph Bowey jnr.*

surfacing, landscaping, haulage, plant hire and car and van hire.

All the many businesses operated with their own trading names, and at the Group's peak in the 1970s it employed some 1,200 staff. But in reality growth was not as straight forward as it may seem in retrospect. There have been huge peaks and troughs in the building industry over the years - most markedly in the 1970s - when from its peak a sudden recession in the industry saw staff numbers rapidly cut by half to 600 in six months

fleets of building plant in the area. Yet another new company, Gosforth Plant Hire Ltd was a natural development to take on responsibility for the maintenance and economic use of the plant fleet.

Diversification and expansion would continue unabated: a second haulage business was acquired in the 1970s based in St Ann's, near to Tyne Tees Television.

Between 1960 and 1980 the business had changed from having earlier been exclusively a general building contractor. Now just 40 per cent of activity was building contracting, with clients which included local authorities, the NHS and large businesses. Some 15 per cent of effort was being directed to civil engineering building roads and sewers for local authorities, house builders and new towns. An equal proportion of the firm's efforts went into private housebuilding, whilst the remainder of the firm's employees, almost a third, were specialist offering a whole range of services: electrical, plumbing and heating, painting, partitions and ceilings, joinery, metalwork and steel structures, specialist drilling and cutting, road

But even in the 1970s not everything was bad news. In that decade Bowey's established the North's major show jumping venue in the decade and hosted the Junior International Event in 1978.

Ralph Bowey junior died in 1988; his son Ron Bowey who had joined the business in the 1960s had been Chairman since 1985 - one his daughters since became the fourth generation of the Bowey family to work in the company.

Since the 1980s the trend to diversification would be reversed, with most of the subsidiary businesses being sold or closed. That concentration of effort would enable the premises to be consolidated. In 1990 the Group left its post-war home in South Gosforth for brand new premises in the up and coming Newcastle Business Park where

Top left: *Bowey built the new research block above the RVI in 1967.* ***Right:*** *A Ministerial visit to the Prince's Building development in Newcastle's historic Quayside area in the mid 1980s.* ***Below:*** *A Bowey Group exhibition stand in the late 1960s.* ***Below right:*** *The extended offices at William Street with staff and their families on an open day.*

16,000 sq ft of office space was built, mostly for the use of the Bowey Group.

By 2000 the Homes and Construction elements of the business had been separated fully; though still being part of the Bowey Group Ltd: Bowey Homes Ltd now moved its base to Team Valley.

In the first year of the new millennium the Group had achieved a turnover of almost £50 million. Core businesses were in building contracting and housing. Building contracting by Bowey Construction Ltd would cover all sectors in the North East, though with a particular emphasis on schools and other educational institutions. Bowey Homes Ltd concentrated on private housing developments across the North east, mainly three and four-bedroomed detached homes, but including a number of upmarket apartment schemes.

In the new century the Group still includes two specialist businesses: Ward Electrical and a newcomer, Bowey (PFI) Ltd. Ward Electrical mainly services the leisure sector across the whole UK whilst Bowey (PFI) is a 'facilities management' company based in Northumberland, looking after the Northumbria Mounted Police Section.

In 2002 Bowey Construction Ltd was sold to its management team in an 'MBO' -Management Buy Out - leaving the Bowey Group to focus on private housing developments across the region from Alnwick in the North to Teesside in the South and Hexham in the West. The Group now employs just 150 staff and has a turnover of half what had previously been experienced - far more significantly however, and surprisingly to outsiders, as a focused housebuilder the profits of the remaining core business miraculously increased by 50 per cent!

Consciously aiming to stand out from the crowd Bowey has become known as the quality home builder that really cares about its customers. Countless developments, buildings and homes, have been integrated into prestigious locations around the North: each new project has been given careful attention, not least by giving full consideration to every building's surroundings.

In the 21st century the name Bowey has become synonymous with quality homes: it's an enviable position, and one which founder, Ralph Bowey senior, would certainly have been immensely proud of.

Top right: *Staff taking part in a raft race when the 'Tall Ships' came to Newcastle in the mid 1980s.* ***Left:*** *Ron Bowey's youngest daughter, Rebecca, presents HRH Prince Philip with a commemorative gift on the occasion of him opening the firm's new premises on February 15th 1991.* ***Below left:*** *The North Haven development of 500 apartments and houses in Sunderland completed in 2000.* ***Below:*** *Ron Bowey.*

Light at the end of the tunnel

Once upon a time miners stuck candles on the brims of their hard hats: it wasn't a very safe practice. Two centuries ago the famous Davy safety lamp, was introduced, whose metal gauze cover did so much to reduce the danger of explosion from flammable gases. But these days Newcastle's Victor company provides even safer lighting in hazardous environments.

Victor Products, now based at Newcastle's New York Way industrial park, was founded in 1929 to supply drilling equipment and hazardous area equipment, including lighting, cable couplers and connectors to the mining industry. Using its long-established experience Victor has since also developed the technology to produce equipment for a wide range of hazardous areas above ground, including the petrochemical, oil and gas industry.

The company was founded as Charles Crofton and Company (Engineers) Ltd based in Wallsend. The two prime movers were a pair of engineers, Harold B Crofton and Reginald W Mann. To begin with there was only a staff of five: an office was rented from British Engines Ltd in Glasshouse Street, St Peters, Newcastle.

Harold Crofton, local to the North East, had previously worked as a design engineer and later ran an agency business, begun by his father Charles Crofton, for such items as mining pumps, winding engines, brake linings and wire ropes. Reg Mann from Birmingham had been a mining electrical engineer and held a senior position with a company selling mining equipment. On 26th July 1929 this pair floated the new company with £1,500, with its object to design develop and market electric rotary drills and ancillary equipment as well as flameproof plugs and sockets for use in coal mines.

Today's company name, Victor, first made its appearance in 1931 as the name of a rotary electric drill newly developed by Crofton and Mann for use on coal and stone. In the meantime workings in mines were undergoing major change: conveyors, coal cutters and other machinery were being introduced. Charles Crofton & Co Ltd directed its skills towards the design, development and sale of electrical plugs and sockets. For the first time a British company was successfully marketing advanced mining equipment in the face of strong competition from foreign firms. It was now that the Ardeloy drilling bit which the company subsequently sold in millions leapt into prominence: until then drilling bits had mainly been manufactured by Krupps of Germany. In the light of subsequent events Britain would be very fortunate in no longer having to rely on German parts. By 1935 company turnover had reached £40,514. By 1937 turnover had risen to £90,000 and the workforce to 56. By the outbreak of war in 1939 the workforce had reached 127.

The company had also begun making flameproof equipment for the mining industry in 1936, products which continued to be made during the course of the second world war. During the war years between 1939 and 1945 almost two thirds of output was in the form of aircraft components, tank tracks, shell discs, valves for battleships, glider release devices and other components.

The importance of the company's contribution to the UK war effort had not been missed by the Germans. An aerial photograph of the factory was found by

***Top left:** Co-founder Harold B Crofton. **Top right:** Co-founder Reginald W Mann. **Left:** One of the first Victor Coal Drills issued to Lambton, Hetton and Joicey Collieries, 1933.*

allied forces in a German air field in occupied Belgium: happily, like the German drill bits, the Luftwaffe just wasn't good enough - the nearest bomb dropped 200 yards wide of its target.

In April 1944, during the course of the war, Harold Crofton retired and took up an appointment with the Ministry of Supply. Reg Mann and a number of senior employees bought out Crofton's shares and three months later the company was renamed Victor Products (Wallsend) Ltd after its best known product.

Part way through the war it had been realised nationally just how important coal production was to the overall war effort. As a result the company was encouraged to gradually switch back to its original work. As a consequence the end of the war in 1945 found Victor Products firmly established in the home market, and poised to begin exporting. In the late 1940s Victor would begin large scale exports of drilling machinery to India, Czechoslovakia and Poland - in each case the largest such export orders ever received in the UK up to that time.

THIS CERTIFIES

that the FLAME-PROOF ENCLOSURE of a
30 Ampere "Victor" Plug and Socket Connector,
for voltages up to 650 volts, with electrical
interlock for remote control circuit,
DESIGNED IN ACCORDANCE WITH THE ATTACHED DRAWINGS 74, 76, 77 and 78, dated 1st April, 15th April, 26th April and 3rd May, 1932, respectively, and SUBMITTED BY CHARLES CROFTON AND COMPANY (ENGINEERS) LIMITED, of WHITLEY BAY,
has been tested at the Mines Department Testing Station, Buxton,
and that
WITH RESPECT TO INFLAMMABLE ATMOSPHERES CONTAINING
FIREDAMP (METHANE)
IT COMPLIES WITH THE DEFINITION OF FLAME-PROOF ENCLOSURE IN BRITISH STANDARD SPECIFICATION No. 229-1929, under the conditions described in the Test Report which has been supplied to Charles Crofton and Company (Engineers) Limited.

H.M. Electrical Inspector of Mines.

On behalf of the Secretary for Mines.

DEFINITION OF FLAME-PROOF ENCLOSURE (INCLUDING EXPLOSION-PROOF) FOR ELECTRICAL APPARATUS.
Part I. of British Standard Specification No. 229-1929: Flame-proof Enclosures for Electrical Apparatus.

A Flame-proof Enclosure (including explosion-proof, for electrical apparatus is one which will withstand, without injury, any explosion that may occur in practice within it under the conditions of operation within the rating of the apparatus enclosed by it (and recognised overloads, if any, associated therewith), and will prevent the transmission of flame such as will ignite any inflammable mixture which may be present in the surrounding atmosphere.

CERTIFICATE No. FLP. 49.
M.S. 5230/32.
12th May, 1932.

The first flame proof electric light had been produced for the mining, oil and gas industries in 1946; it would be the forerunner of a range of products which would eventually become responsible for almost a third of the company's sales.

By the end of 1950 factory and office space had grown from the original 8,240 sq ft to some 50,800 sq ft. The company had its own foundry, machine shop, assembly shop, tool room, diecasting shop, process department, test and inspection department, pattern making and electricians shops, as well as a spacious research and development area. The labour force was now 375 and annual turnover had reached half a million pounds.

The business became a public limited company, quoted on the London Stock exchange, in 1955 under the name Victor Products (Wallsend) Ltd.

Above: *The first Flameproof Certificate issued in 1932 to the company.* ***Below:*** *An aerial view of the works.* ***Inset:*** *An early view of the office.*

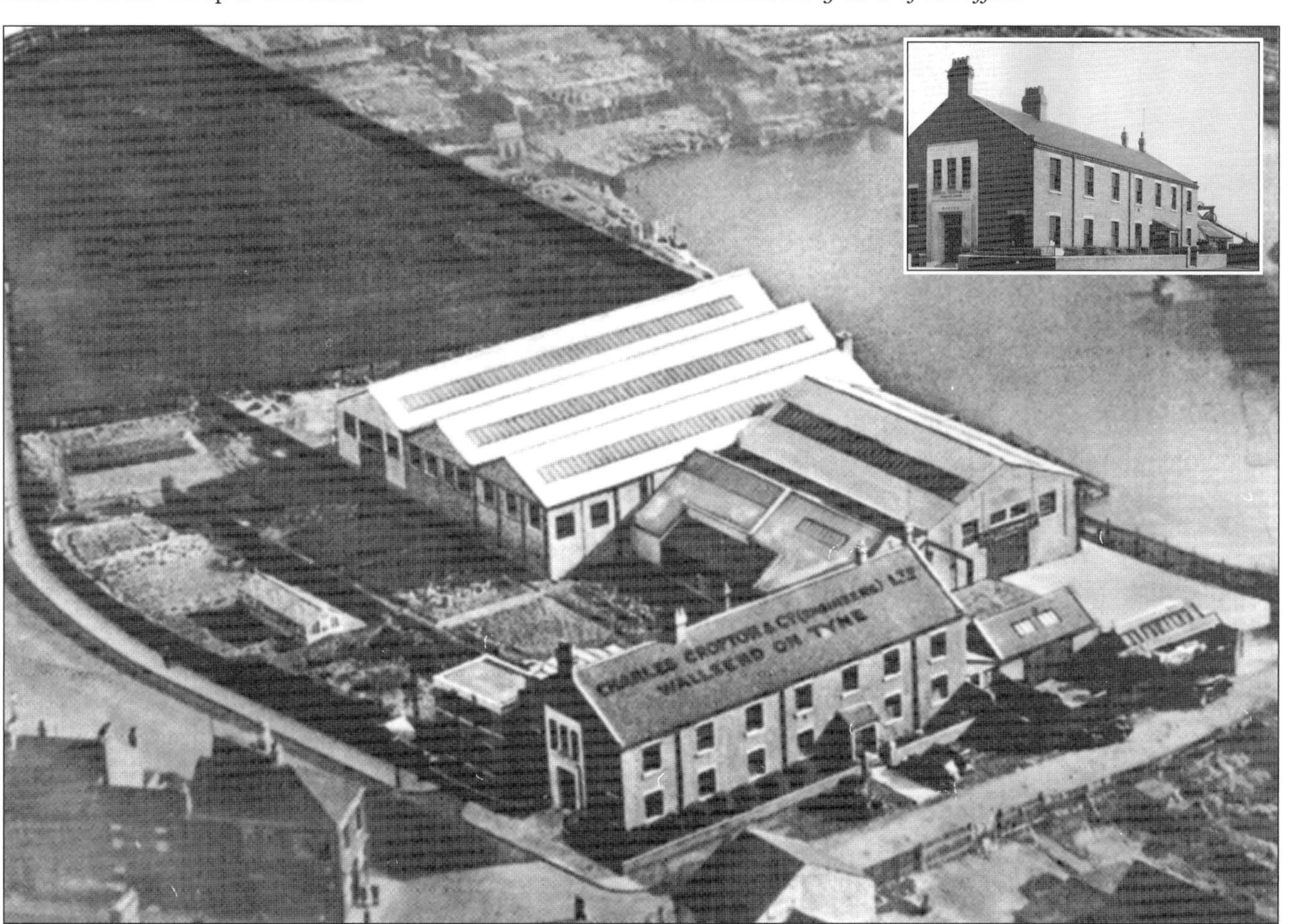

By 1958 the company's export market extended to 86 countries and the workforce had expanded to 450 - and in the process achieved an annual turnover of more than one million pounds for the first time.

Gradual recession in the coal mining industry would however now begin to make inroads into the company's success: some staff were made redundant and sales would remain static or worse for several years. But it would not all be bad news. One massive order for 3,000 sets of drilling equipment was received from China, whilst in 1962 the company entered the market for petrol pump lighting, becoming the main supplier of such lighting in the UK. Petrol pump lighting would lead to the development of lighting for other semi-hazardous locations and the range would be extended by the successful introduction of weatherproof and vapourproof fittings.

In 1964 Jardine Victor Ltd was formed in India, a jointly owned company created to manufacture Victor products locally. Nearer home at Westoe Colliery, South Shields, the first full lighting system for a mechanised coal face was installed by Victor as well as extensive roadway illumination. Thousands of similar fittings would follow.

In order to cope with now increasing demand land adjoining the works was acquired in 1970, the existing works buildings were extended to provide some 125,000 sq ft in total.

Transtar joined the Victor group in 1973 manufacturing control gear for lighting including Victor's flameproof 'luminaires'. Transtar, founded in 1947 as Inductive Appliances, had been Victors largest supplier, now continuity of supplies to Victor were assured.

The company continued its expansion and in 1976 opened a second purpose-built factory on Middle Engine Lane to accomodate the manufacturing of drilling equipment.

Meanwhile the development of North Sea oil was producing new markets for the company's products. Shortage of production space led to the lightng side of the business moving to 84,000 sq ft factory premises on Norham Road in 1978. Huge exports to both Poland and China in that year underscored the wisdom of the move.

Top: *An interior view of the works.* ***Above:*** *A section of the Stenographers Department.* ***Left:*** *An underground roadway using Victor incandescent lighting.*

By now turnover had reached a staggering £10 million and the workforce had risen to 900. The following year a South African subsidiary was formed - Victor Industrial Equipment (Proprietary) Ltd and in May 1982 Victor Products USA was established.

Celebrating its half century in 1979 the company was however still a family firm despite its remarkable growth: the Chairman and Managing Director was LR Mann, the nephew of the co-founder, who had joined Victor in 1955 before becoming Managing Director in 1965 after having occupied several other roles.

The first of the radically designed Excalibur range of 'luminaires' was launched in 1983. The following year Victor would lead the UK in manufacturing technology with the installation of the first Flexible Manufacturing System.

Victor became part of the United States-owned Federal Signal Corporation (FSC), a billion dollar corporation listed on the New York Stock

Exchange, in 1996. The following year Victor relocated to a purpose-built 6,500 sqm factory in New York, Newcastle Upon Tyne.

With over seven decades of experience in manufacturing hazardous area equipment to the highest standards of quality and reliability Victor has developed the technology to produce innovative lighting solutions which are used and relied upon in the most arduous of environments across the whole world.

Today the Victor Group, with bases in the USA, the Middle East, South Africa - and not forgetting Newcastle - aims to be the first choice supplier of electrical products for all hazardous and industrial environments.

Top left: *Petrol pumps fitted with Victor safety lighting.* ***Top right:*** *Lighting on the Salvesen Offshore Drilling Ltd Drill Ship.* ***Left:*** *Reginald Mann shows the O.B.E. to his wife after he had received it from H.M the Queen at the Investiture at the Palace.* ***Below:*** *The Lord Lieutenant of Tyne and Wear, Sir James Steel, presenting the Queen's Award for Technological Achievement to Mr L R Mann, who received the award on behalf of the company in 1976.*

The centre of shopping

There have been shops, at least of a sort, in Newcastle since the first open markets were held here uncounted centuries ago. By Victorian times those temporary stalls, once set up in fields, had long since disappeared to be replaced by streets filled with glass-fronted shops built of imposing stone, shops which many readers will still remember, and many fine examples of which still survive. Indeed readers over the age of forty will have no difficulty recalling a quite different style of shopping in Newcastle from that which exists today - especially getting wet when it rained!

In the 1970s we thought we already knew everything worth knowing about shops and shopping, but more than thirty years ago something quite new to our experience began to arise in the city centre.

In 1976 Newcastle Upon Tyne's city centre was changed forever by the opening of a new multi-million pound shopping centre - Eldon Square - a development which today covers some ten acres of Newcastle City Centre. It is owned 40 per cent by the City, and the remainder is split equally between the Shell Pension Trust and CSC PLC - Capital Shopping Centres.

Above: *Eldon Square under construction in the early 1970s.* ***Right:*** *An aerial view of the development.* ***Below:*** *Eldon Square before building work began.*

Building work on the F-shaped development had begun in 1973, with a design brief which included not only a large number of shops but also a bus concourse, offices, a new market and car parking. The architects were Chapman Taylor Partners.

The project, which cost £60 million, resulted in one of the largest covered shopping centres in Europe, by far the largest in Britain. The scale was astonishing and eventually resulted in almost a million square feet of retail space containing some 148 shops; catering outlets alone offer seats for 1,300 customers not to mention the centre's 1,800 car parking spaces and the fact that it provides employment for 4,000 people. This was a development which astonished not just Newcastle but the whole region.

Due to its size and complexity the Centre opened in phases. Phase one opened on 4th March 1976 and included the Greenmarket. Shops never seen in the city before now moved in.

Phase two opened six months later and included Boots and Bainbridge (now John Lewis) as well as integrating the already existing Fenwick and Marks & Spencer stores.

Over the years the Eldon Square shopping

centre has played host to some of the most popular celebrities and sports personalities of the day including 'the Greatest' boxer Muhammad Ali and tennis star Bjorn Borg - and was also honoured by several royal visits. Her Majesty the Queen unveiled a commemorative clock during her Jubilee Year of 1977. The clock remains high on the wall in Chevy Chase, a timely reminder to passing shoppers. Her Majesty Queen Elizabeth, the late Queen Mother, was also a visitor.

Eldon Square has however not rested on its laurels. In 1988 an extensive refurbishment opened up many ceiling areas, creating new atriums with new lighting and signage. The following year an ambitious extension provided an extra 80,000 square feet in the south side of the Centre - the new Newgate Mall including a Food Court, extra mall space for new shops and a link to the south end of the city.

The 1990s brought even more change to Eldon Square - not least when in October 1990 Sunday shopping came to the Centre, an innovation which since then has been increasingly popular.

Since its opening in 1976 countless millions of happy shoppers have passed through the doors of the Eldon Square shopping centre. And the use of the word 'millions' is no exaggeration: the Centre has more than 25 million visitors each year - 70,000 coming from as far way as Scandinavia so famous has Newcastle become as the place to do some serious shopping.

A whole generation has now grown up in Newcastle knowing no other cityscape than the one which contains the Eldon Square Shopping Centre. For oldies Eldon Square may still be 'that new shopping place' but for Newcastle's young adults this is now what the city centre has always looked like, and slowly but inexorably Eldon Square is becoming part of the city's rich architectural heritage.

***This page:** Various aspects of the Eldon Square Shopping Centre including the celebrations held to commemorate the 25th Anniversary of the centre in 2001.*

Are you being served

The centre of Newcastle has been famed for the quality of its shops for longer than any reader can possibly recall. Of course there have been, and still are, many different kinds of shop. There are many small family owned businesses trading alongside huge chain stores representing nationally renowned firms.

But as we all learned in our schooldays mighty oaks grow from tiny acorns. Some of today's small businesses may themselves grow to become famous chains. And equally some of today's mighty commercial giants started their lives as small businesses run by one man.

In 2002, after 164 years in the city, one of Newcastle's most familiar shops, Bainbridge, finally changed its name to John Lewis. Not before time some said, after all the John Lewis Partnership had bought the Bainbridge store half a century earlier.

Today the John Lewis Partnership is one of Britain's leading retail businesses. Astonishingly to those not in the know the business belongs to all those who work within it on a permanent basis; those staff are known as 'partners' from the day they join. The firm has no outside shareholders: all the ordinary share capital is held by John Lewis Trustees on behalf of all the partners, who each get a share of any profits made each year as well as a say in how the business is run.

The John Lewis story really began in 1864 when the original John Lewis, then a young draper from Somerset who had arrived in London in 1856 with just a single golden guinea (£1.05) in his pocket. He opened a small drapers shop which he developed into a department store, located, as it still is today, in London's Oxford Street. The first day's takings amounted to just one pound. Success came gradually, but John Lewis gained a reputation for honesty and for having the largest selection of goods in the West End. In 1905 John Lewis also bought the Peter Jones department store in Sloane Square to expand the business.

John Lewis had two sons, Spedan and Oswald: on his sons' twenty-first birthdays he gave each of them a quarter share in the business, making it a family concern. Oswald Lewis left the firm in 1925 to join the legal profession, later becoming an MP: but he returned in 1951 as its Director of Financial Operations.

John Spedan Lewis had a strong social conscience, and very early had noticed that the income the Lewis family was drawing from the business was more than the whole of their 300 employees combined. This fact disturbed Spedan and he began a lifelong process of dividing the business rewards more equally - not something that 'Old John' approved of in the slightest.

In 1914 control of Peter Jones had been given to John Spedan Lewis and it was there that he first experimented with sharing information and responsibilities between management and the managed, developing a Committee for Communication, a Staff Council and an in-house magazine.

On inheriting both shops from his father, who died at the age of 92 in 1928, Spedan Lewis, began the remarkable process of transferring the

***Above:** An artist's impression of Bainbridge's premises in the early 1900s.* ***Right:** John Lewis, founder of an empire.*

business into the hands of its employees. Meanwhile the business continued to grow: by the early years of the second world war 18 further department stores had been acquired, as well as the Waitrose chain of foodshops which had been bought in 1937.

In 1950 Spedan Lewis gave his voting rights to Trustees and set up a written constitution securing the structure of the partnership, giving democratic responsibilities and making management accountable to the non-management partners.

Top: *Bainbridge's store decorated for the coronation of King George VI in 1937.* ***Above:*** *A Bainbridge delivery van from the early 1900s.* ***Right:*** *A garden party at Espley Hall in 1911.*

It was at this stage in its history that in 1952 the John Lewis Partnership acquired Newcastle's historic Bainbridge store, a business founded by the delightfully named Emerson Muschamp Bainbridge.

At the age of 13 in 1830 Emerson Muschamp Bainbridge began serving his time as an apprentice draper before later going off to London for two years. He returned to Newcastle in 1837 and after a brief partnership with William Dunn, a draper of Albert House, Market Street, began working on his own. By 1841 the young entrepreneur was trading in the city as EM Bainbridge from 12 Market Street, and four years later, having taken his cousin Muschamp into partnership, he was employing ten staff. Over the following years neighbouring premises were acquired by Bainbridge and by 1849 he had 23 departments operating both in his original premises and from what had previously been the old stables of the Turks Head Hotel.

Bainbridge had seen that despite the changes brought by the industrial revolution the way people in Newcastle

bought both their necessities and luxuries had altered little since medieval times. Shopping as we know it today was effectively introduced to Newcastle by Bainbridge: he abolished the age old custom of haggling over the cost of goods and brought in fixed prices displayed on tickets.

It was the right place and the right time. Nineteenth century Newcastle was one of the world's fastest growing cities with a young population and an increasingly affluent middle class: they all wanted new and stylish ways of shopping and Bainbridge was only too keen to provide them with it.

By 1865 Bainbridge had bought the stretch of buildings, over 500 feet long with a mile and a half of aisles, running back to Bigg Market. In 1880 factories in Leeds were added to what was becoming the Bainbridge commercial empire.

Emerson Muschamp Bainbridge died in 1892. By the time of his death he had acquired several factories which manufactured hats, shoes, women's clothing, knitted stockings, men's and boys' clothing and mattresses. The factories employed 860 staff and the Newcastle establishment employed 600. Annual sales at the Newcastle store, rebuilt on four stories in 1876, were by now close to £600,000, a fabulous sum in those days. The store was one of the largest shops in the country with more than five acres of shop floor space. On his death the founder's sons became Directors whilst some of his grandsons had by then also joined the family firm.

For the first half of the 20th century Bainbridge & Co Ltd would continue to dominate shopping in Newcastle. The firm was ever eager to adopt new techniques and technology: the first of a fleet of Bainbridge motor delivery vehicles arrived in 1901, and by 1911 the store's already well established mail order department could take orders through a five line telephone switchboard.

Top left: *Bainbridge's premises pictured in 1936.* ***Top right:*** *Bainbridge's menswear department.* ***Above right:*** *GV Muschamp Bainbridge.* ***Right:*** *The modern John Lewis store in the Eldon Centre, Newcastle.*

Celebrating its centenary in 1938 the store announced with chilling foresight that its floor space could provide a parade ground in which 60,000 troops could be drilled in comfort. Air raid shelters would soon be built in what had until then been the Bainbridge wholesale area - it was 1948 before that facility became a new grocery warehouse.

Meanwhile standards had to be maintained - even during the years of the second world war: while many women were reduced to drawing lines on their legs to give the illusion of stockings, female staff at Bainbridge continued to wear nylons to keep up the store's smart image.

The John Lewis Partnership bought Bainbridge for just over one million pounds in 1953. Mr GVM Bainbridge, the founder's grandson, became sole Managing Director, remaining with the branch for the next 21 years until his retirement in 1974.

In 1976 Bainbridge moved from its old Market Street location to a new department store in the Eldon Square Shopping Centre and the old premises were sold; by then the store was employing 1,130 Partners, occupied some 300,000 sq ft and was enjoying an annual turnover of an incredible £25 million.

Many changes have been seen over the years: the funeral department, gents hairdressing and the food hall have long since gone, but in their place have appeared new shopping opportunities such as the books, gardening and sports departments; new goods and services appearing as customer tastes have changed down the decades. In recent years the John Lewis partnership has also diversified into manufacturing, farming and, most recently, a wine merchants

Today, after more than a century and a half of trading in Newcastle the business continues to prosper. Through its trading polices of honesty, value and assortment it continues to offer its customers excellent service and peace of mind, knowing that in accordance with the policies of both Emerson Bainbridge and John Lewis they have been offered nothing but quality merchandise.

Above, both pictures: *Modern room displays in the store, 2003.* ***Below:*** *Newcastle's John Lewis store in 2003.*

The helping hand of the law

The modern commercial law firms based in the city centre today bear no resemblance to the small practices of a hundred years ago.

Robert Muckle, based at Norham House in New Bridge Street West is a perfect example of how radical the changes have been. Today's partners run a highly successful commercial law firm that is progressive and focused in the delivery of a high quality legal service to an impressive list of businesses across the region. Although modern technology has advanced many of the changes, the partners are proud that they have retained the ethos of their founder and believe, as he did, that they should put something back into the North East community.

When Robert Muckle, then aged just 13, joined the solicitor's firm of JM Criddle in 1896 as an office junior, even he would never have guessed that a century later one of the leading commercial law firms in Newcastle would bear his name. Nor would he have ever dreamt that one day he would become Under Sheriff of Newcastle, and in 1955 be awarded the CBE.

Robert Muckle was an ambitious young man who took his articles in 1910 before qualifying as a solicitor five years later. By then the firm was known as Criddle & Criddle and based in Collingwood Street. In 1920 Robert was made a partner and the firm became Criddle, Ord & Muckle. Some years later, his son Leslie Muckle also joined the partnership. In 1951 John Hall became a partner and he was responsible for moving the firm to Norham House in New Bridge Street West. It was considered a radical move at the time as the main business centre of Newcastle was based in Collingwood Street. In 1959, the Criddles left and the firm changed its name to Robert Muckle, Son and Hall.

Not many people today realise that Robert Muckle was one of the first Newcastle lawyers to become a specialist in company law. Although the firm never opened a London office his expertise was well known in the south, and he travelled to London for three days every fortnight in order to conduct business with his southern clients.

One of Robert Muckle's clients, Wilfred Handley, was an industrial chemist based in Byker, who had invented products such as Domestos and Stergene. Robert helped Handley set up his own company and patent his products: when Handley sold out to Unilever he became a millionaire. Wilfred Handley then set up the WA Handley Charity Trust, which is still in operation today helping numerous local charities.

The modern law firm bearing Robert Muckle's name is today a sharply-focused commercial firm. In the final decade of the 20th century and in the opening years of the new millennium its reputation has gone from strength to strength, and the firm enjoys an excellent client base of successful private and public companies.

Above: *Company founder, Robert Muckle, Under Sheriff of Newcastle upon Tyne, 1934.*

In the words of Senior Partner Ian Gilthorpe "The firm is proactive and committed to adding value to clients' businesses. We have a young partnership and it is the innovation and enterprise of our partners that ensures that the firm continues to respond rapidly to changing market conditions - which is exactly the same philosophy adopted by our founder Robert Muckle".

Robert Muckle was awarded his CBE for his services to the community, and today's firm is continuing his good work. Managing Partner, Hugh Welch says,"At Robert Muckle we believe that our success and profitability must not be looked at in isolation from the wider North East community and that we need to play a real part in building a more inclusive society".

In 2002 the partners set up the Robert Muckle Charitable Fund with the Community Foundation to make awards to many local charities and community projects. The firm's partners and staff are encouraged to use their legal skills to help local charities and to become school governors: they have also supported the arts and youth projects, including the development of the Newcastle Cricket Centre at South Northumberland Cricket Club.

In recognition of all its community work, Robert Muckle was presented with the 'Tyneside & Northumberland Business in the Community Award 2002' in March 2003 and was also presented with Business in the Community Award 2002 at the prestigious regional final at Hardwick Hall in May 2003.

There can be no doubt that the firm's founder would have been proud of his successors' continuing adherence to his principles.

Below: *Setting up the Robert Muckle Charitable Fund at the Community Foundation. Pictured from left to right: Hugh Welch (managing partner), Tony McPhillips (Robert Muckle), Barbara Gubbins (Community Foundation), Robert Phillips (Robert Muckle), George Hepburn (Community Foundation), Jonathan Combe (Robert Muckle), Ian Gilthorpe (senior partner).*

Travelling right

"Majorca? Why, what do you want to go there for? When I were a lad we used to have half a day out at Whitley Bay and were glad of it. Mind you the weather was better then."

We all know that the weather was far warmer and the sun stayed in the sky longer in the days of our youth than they do today. And the ice-creams were colder and the donkeys faster too! You've got to go a long way these days to recapture the summer heat of childhood: many of us go looking for it around the Mediterranean or even further afield.

But before then we need to find a travel agent: one of the best is to be found in Gosforth.

'The Travel Bureau' was started by John and Rose Scott in January 1962 with just one employee. That first year turnover was £44,000. Twenty years later turnover had soared to £4 million and the Scotts needed to employ more than 20 staff to keep up with demand.

In setting out on their new enterprise John and Rose were absolutely convinced of two things: first that there really was a need for an up-to-date travel bureau in Gosforth and secondly that Gosforth folk would not accept an inferior service.

After serving in the forces during the second world war John Scott had gone into the motor business eventually employing 20 men, but ill health forced him to sell up and look for a different career. Though John knew nothing about the travel industry Rose knew pretty well everything worth knowing about running a travel bureau - not least never to deal with dubious or doubtful operators. If any untrustworthy operator did evade Rose's black list she never allowed a firm to let The Travel Bureau or its clients down twice!

***Top left:** John and Rose Scott pictured in the 1960s. **Above right:** The Travel Bureau at 69/71 High Street. **Far right:** Inside The Travel Bureau in the early 1960s. **Right:** The Travel Bureau at 61 High Street.*

It was a tough policy, and indeed one that once got John hauled in front of ABTA for refusing to deal with one local tour operator which subsequently collapsed. Such publicity however did nothing but enhance The Travel Bureau's reputation for straight dealing.

In 1962 The Travel Bureau was located behind a record shop at 61 High Street Gosforth; at the end of the first year the firm took over the whole of the premises. Eight years later such was the demand for the bureau's services that it moved to its present, and much larger, premises at 69/71 High Street. By 1974 the company turned over £1 million pounds. In 1976 John Scott Jnr joined the company, after a successful career in the motor trade, and started to learn the business closely in 1968.

The company kept on expanding both the retail and business travel departments and in 1988 John Jnr and Jeff Bell took over the running of the company via a management buyout, although John Snr and Rose were still actively involved with the company until John Snr passed away in September 1990 and Rose in August 1993.

The premises were completely gutted and refurbished in 1991 much to the surprise of staff and customers alike. The company remained opened during the whole period of renovation which lasted a whole month, with contractors working 24 hours a day.

John and Jeff, with the invaluable help of a team of very loyal and experienced staff, have continued to take the business forward to a peak turnover in 2000 of some £12.9 million pounds. Today, at the start of the new millennium, the travel bureau continues with the same principles started by John and Rose, some forty years ago, of providing a professional and individual service to all of its clients using the full spectrum of modern technology from the purchase of rail tickets to a first class round the world itinerary tailor-made to the clients needs.

Above: *Jeffrey Bell, left and John Scott, Directors of the company.* ***Left and below:*** *Inside The Travel Bureau, 2003.*

Property is their business

Any issue connected with property can present difficulties. Happily, with over 125 staff Storey Sons & Parker - the largest independent Chartered Surveying practice in the North of England - can help.

George H Storey was born at the Old Farm near Gosforth Station, he decided to set up on his own in 1891. George Storey's first offices were previously the studio of the famous local portrait painters John Storey and John Hodgson Campbell. The building was demolished in the 1920s to make way for the Super Cinema owned by Paramount Theatres and which later become the Odeon cinema.

Russell Storey joined his father in 1905; the firm now became known as Geo. H Storey & Son. The 'son' became 'sons' in 1912 when the founder's younger son, Winship Storey, joined the firm. That same year the firm moved to new offices at 1 Higham Place.

In 1930 the trio were joined by Robert Parker: he was Honorary Secretary of the Northumberland and Durham branch of the Chartered Auctioneers and Estate Agents Institute of which Russell Storey was branch chairman.

With the arrival of Robert Parker the firm changed its name yet again: to Geo. H Storey Sons & Parker; it now had a staff of 17. Ron Scott joined the firm in 1942 and soon left, only to return for a four year stint in 1948, the year Stuart Sisterson arrived, before leaving again to spend the next 15 years in Nigeria before returning for good in 1963.

Founder George Storey died in 1949 at the age of 85; he was a lifelong Methodist and had been a member of the Salters Road Methodist Church.

Two years later Robert Parker who had been a Councillor for Newcastle's Dene Ward since 1949 was elected Deputy Lord mayor of the City.

The death of the firm's founder left a gap which would be filled in 1955 when Robert Parker took both his son Howard Parker and Stuart Sisterson into partnership. Two more partners Bob Edmonds and Tony Thwaites joined in 1959 and 1960 respectively.

In July of 1960 the partnership acquired the London firm of Way & Waller; this was perhaps the first ever instance of a provincial firm taking over a London one.

The 1960s was an era of change. In 1961 the firm amalgamated with Anderson

***Top left:** Robert Parker, 1962. **Above right:** Stuart Sisterson, 1962. **Right:** The firm's premises pictured in 1961.*

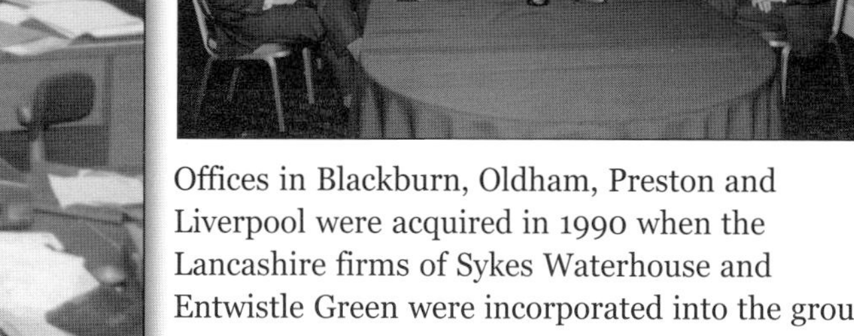

Offices in Blackburn, Oldham, Preston and Liverpool were acquired in 1990 when the Lancashire firms of Sykes Waterhouse and Entwistle Green were incorporated into the group.

In 1991 a management buy-out, led by Nick Blezard, Ian Battle, Kevan Carrick, John Irwin, Bill Lynn and Martyn Lytollis, was completed. At the time SS&P had 137 employees and an annual turnover of £3 million.

By the early years of the 21st century Storey Sons & Parker had evolved into a multi-disciplinary firm of chartered surveyors and commercial property consultants with offices in Newcastle, Teesside, Leeds and Manchester. But though many changes have occurred since the firm was founded in 1891 George Storey's personal commitment to quality, expertise and reputation remains unaltered.

and Garland another Newcastle firm of auctioneers estate agents and valuers, in the process taking Jack Bernasconi of that firm into partnership. Two more partners Bob Edmonds and Ron Scott appeared in 1963 on the death of Robert Parker at the age of 65.

Work began on new premises on the same site in 1965; the work would take three years to complete, sadly during the building work Howard Parker died at the age of only 35 whilst playing tennis at the Gosforth Club. The new offices, Higham House in New Bridge Street West, finally opened in 1968.

Top left: *The office in the late 1960s.* ***Above left:*** *Robert H Parker.* ***Top right:*** *The Partners in 1986.* ***Below:*** *The Directors pictured in 2003.*

Branches opened in 1970 and 1972 in Middlesbrough and Darlington. Russell J Storey died aged 83, in September 1972. In the late 1970s offices opened in Stokesley and Morpeth.

Kevan Carrick and John Irwin were appointed partners in 1981 and Bill Lynn and Ian Battle in 1986 on the retirement of Stuart Sisterson.

Martyn Lytollis became partner in 1988, a year of major change. In 1988 'SS&P' was taken over by Black Horse Agencies and the company gained eight offices in Teesside and North Yorkshire. A Leeds office was opened the following year.

Building a reputation

The building industry is a notoriously fickle mistress. A glance through the business gazetteers of yesteryear easily demonstrates how quickly building firms come and go; they are optimistically created during times when the economy is rising but they tend to disappear just as quickly, going bust when the inevitable downturn arrives.

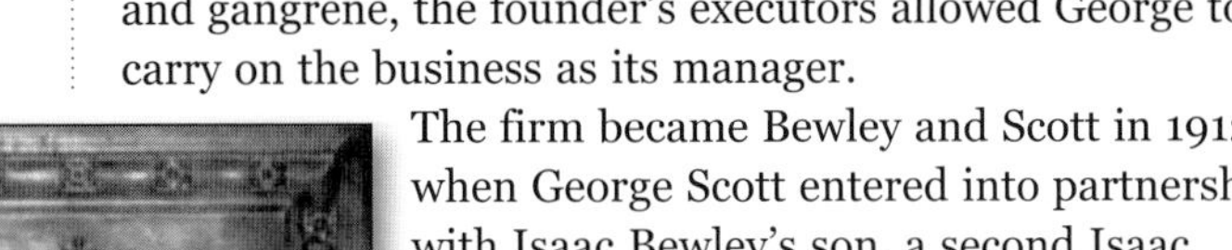

Hundreds of small firms have come and gone: the unsuccessful ones have fallen by the wayside - and the few successful ones have all too often been snatched up by larger firms.

But astonishingly at least one local family run building firm has survived the stormy economic seas for more than a hundred years: Bewley & Scott Ltd.

The business, now based in Ellison Road, Dunston, was founded in 1892 when Isaac Bewley (1862 - 1906) a native of Belford in Northumberland began trading in Newcastle as a builder and undertaker.

George Vickers Scott (1883-1956) started work for Isaac Bewley in 1899 when he was 16 years old at a time when Bewley was in the process of building the imposing St Chad's Church in Bensham. When Isaac Bewley died in Newcastle General Hospital after suffering from peritonitis and gangrene, the founder's executors allowed George to carry on the business as its manager.

The firm became Bewley and Scott in 1912 when George Scott entered into partnership with Isaac Bewley's son, a second Isaac Bewley.

Both George Vickers Scott and Isaac Bewley junior served as officers in the first world war; the business was left to be run by a manager, George Reed, until George Scott was discharged from the army in 1919 after recovering from wounds.

Sadly Isaac Bewley was not to return having been killed just one month before the end of the conflict which took the lives of so many other men from Newcastle and all around the world. George Scott now bought Isaac's share of the company from his widow, Edith Bewley, but continued to trade as Bewley & Scott.

The business was formed into a limited company in 1920 with just two shareholders: George Scott and Stephen Eastern. (Stephen Eastern, later Sir Stephen and Lord Mayor of Newcastle, had in fact been one of the founder's close friends and executors). Eastern would however eventually sell his share of the company to George Scott which in 1937 left him as Chairman and Managing Director, positions which he retained until his death in 1956.

Above: *The plaque in St Chad's Church, commemorating Isaac Bewley.* ***Right:*** *St Chad's Church, Bensham.* ***Below:*** *Replacement windmill blades for Whitburn Windmill.*

Until the late 1930s the company concentrated on building houses. As the business developed however more industrial and commercial building was taken on, including hospitals and churches.

Following George Scott's death Wilf Ward, who had started work for Bewley & Scott in 1919, became Managing Director, he remained so until 1969 by which time he had completed half a century with the company. Such long service was not unique: Mr R Mallams who had begun working for the company in 1920 and became company secretary ten years later would also complete his own 50 years marathon before retiring in 1970. Meanwhile George Scott's widow Mrs MA Scott had been Chairman of the company since her husband's death; she was assisted on the board of directors by her son George Rodney Scott who would in turn become chairman in 1977 on his mother's death.

Charles Vickers Scott who had become Managing Director in 1970 would in his turn become Chairman in 1986 on the death of George Rodney Scott.

In the opening decade of the 21st century long service and family involvement continue to be an outstanding feature of Bewley & Scott: Chairman Charles Vickers passed the 50 year tape in 1999, John Vickers Scott who started work in 1971 became Managing Director in 1994 whilst company secretary John Stobbart had been with the firm since 1955 and would complete more than 40 years before retiring. Other board members Betty May Scott, Alan Rochelle, Gary Smith and Gary McCaughey, who succeeded John Stobbart as Company Secretary on his retirement, were equally long serving or aspiring to it.

Today this long-lived building company still continues the traditions that have already served it well for eleven decades, still offering skills and standards of workmanship that it is confident will help ensure that the firm continues to thrive as it moves into its second century.

Top left: *An aerial view of the firm's site.* ***Top right:*** *Oldwell Surgery, Winlaton.* ***Above:*** *St Nicholas Church, Dunston.* ***Right:*** *Directors and staff outside the premises in 2003.*

Higher, longer, deeper

Based at St Ann's Wharf, Quayside, Newcastle's Mott MacDonald is today a world class, multi-disciplinary engineering and management consultancy. The company is engaged in developments which touch many parts of everyday life - from transport and energy, building, water and the environment, industry, communications, to education and social development.

When railway and dock specialist Basil Mott and mining engineer David Hay became partners in 1902 little could they have imagined that they were the forerunners of a company which would have 7,000 staff world-wide, and an annual turnover of £400 million: the founding pair would have been far too involved in developing the London Underground to have such pipe dreams.

Following the first world war the firm, now Mott, Hay and Anderson (later to become Mott MacDonald), worked on numerous river crossings, not least the Tyne Bridge between Gateshead and Newcastle, - the longest steel arch in Britain when completed in 1928. Six years later the firm was working on the Tees (Newport) vertical lifting bridge - the largest of its kind in the world. As a result of continuing work on the London Underground David Anderson travelled to Moscow to advise on the construction of that city's famous Metro. In that same period the firm also engineered the famous Mersey Tunnel between Liverpool and Birkenhead - at the time another 'largest in the world'.

During the second world war the firm was involved in building air raid shelters and repairing the London underground. Post-war the firm took up bridge building

Right: *The King and Queen arrive at the Tyne Bridge on opening day, 10th October 1928.* ***Below:*** *The bridge taking shape on 12th January 1928.*

again: almost every major civil engineering project in Britain seems to have been touched by the firm: the Dartford Tunnel for example was begun in 1956.

In partnership with the firm of Freeman Fox, Mott MacDonald began work on the Firth of Forth Road Bridge completed in 1958; the work involved not only the 3,300 ft centre span of the bridge, but nine miles of related road works and another 24 bridges.

With Freeman and Fox the firm now moved on to the Severn suspension bridge, opened in 1966, and to the Tamar Bridge linking Cornwall and Devon.

Until the 1960s most work had been in the UK: that was set to change as the firm now moved into mass rapid transit systems and maritime engineering. Maritime work began with platform design in the North Sea, work which soon led to contracts in the Middle East designing a cargo port in Jordan as well as port, rail and road facilities in Iraq.

One of the company's first international offices was in Singapore helping service the Singapore mass transit system - work which would in turn lead to similar work in Melbourne and Helsinki, not to mention preliminary designs for a system to link Newcastle with Gateshead.

Asia would not be the only new continent conquered. When the new London Bridge was designed by the company in the late 1960s the American buyers of the old bridge wanted it removed and rebuilt in Arizona.

Meanwhile in Milan the need to find a new method of drilling below the water table led John Bartlett - later to become company chairman - to invent the 'bentonite shield', a device which saved tunnellers from the rigours of having to work in compressed air: by 1979 no fewer than 35 bentonite shields were at work in Japan alone.

The greatest civil engineering project of the 20th century was the channel tunnel. Mott, Hay and Anderson carried out a feasibility study for the project in 1929. Now Mott MacDonald became principal design consultants for all civil and geotechnical engineering on the UK section.

During the channel tunnel project the firm was leading 500 staff, the work led to the presentation of the 1991 Civil Engineering Award and the 1992 Concrete Society Award.

By the early 1990s the company was expanding at a rapid pace. There were now over 3,000 staff world-wide. At home work on the M3 near Winchester and the A34 Newbury by-pass demonstrated the company's ability to introduce innovative measures to preserve wildlife, control pollution and protect sites of special scientific interest. On the railways the company won contracts to provide engineering services to a range of schemes to improve the West Coast and East Coast main lines as well as being lead designer for the Heathrow Express.

In the USA the company has recently completed multi-lane highway tunnels to remove congestion from Boston's city centre: Back in Newcastle work is well underway on another landmark project The Sage in Gateshead. Mott MacDonald are responsible for most of the engineering including structural and building services design.

Top left: *Constructing of the Channel Tunnel for which Mott MacDonald was TLM's principal design consultant for all civil and geotechnical engineering on the UK section.* ***Below:*** *The Life Interactive building, Mott MacDonald were contracted for the multi disciplinary engineering and infrastructure design, transport planning, geotechnical investigation, construction supervision and planning supervisor.*

Acknowledgments

The publishers would like to thank

Newcastle Central Library

The Ward Philipson Group

Dilys Harding

Ken Hitcham

Andrew Mitchell

Steve Ainsworth

True North Books Ltd - Book List

Memories of Accrington - 1 903204 05 4
Memories of Barnet - 1 903204 16 X
Memories of Barnsley - 1 900463 11 3
Golden Years of Barnsley -1 900463 87 3
Memories of Basingstoke - 1 903204 26 7
Memories of Bedford - 1 900463 83 0
More Memories of Bedford - 1 903204 33 X
Golden Years of Birmingham - 1 900463 04 0
Birmingham Memories - 1 903204 45 3
Memories of Blackburn - 1 900463 40 7
More Memories of Blackburn - 1 900463 96 2
Memories of Blackpool - 1 900463 21 0
Memories of Bolton - 1 900463 45 8
More Memories of Bolton - 1 900463 13 X
Bolton Memories - 1 903204 37 2
Memories of Bournemouth -1 900463 44 X
Memories of Bradford - 1 900463 00 8
More Memories of Bradford - 1 900463 16 4
More Memories of Bradford II - 1 900463 63 6
Bradford Memories - 1 903204 47 X
Bradford City Memories - 1 900463 57 1
Memories of Bristol - 1 900463 78 4
More Memories of Bristol - 1 903204 43 7
Memories of Bromley - 1 903204 21 6
Memories of Burnley - 1 900463 95 4
Golden Years of Burnley - 1 900463 67 9
Memories of Bury - 1 900463 90 3
Memories of Cambridge - 1 900463 88 1
Memories of Cardiff - 1 900463 14 8
Memories of Carlisle - 1 900463 38 5
Memories of Chelmsford - 1 903204 29 1
Memories of Cheltenham - 1 903204 17 8
Memories of Chester - 1 900463 46 6
More Memories of Chester -1 903204 02 X
Memories of Chesterfield -1 900463 61 X
More Memories of Chesterfield - 1 903204 28 3
Memories of Colchester - 1 900463 74 1
Nostalgic Coventry - 1 900463 58 X
Coventry Memories - 1 903204 38 0

Memories of Croydon - 1 900463 19 9
More Memories of Croydon - 1 903204 35 6
Golden Years of Darlington - 1 900463 72 5
Nostalgic Darlington - 1 900463 31 8
Darlington Memories - 1 903204 46 1
Memories of Derby - 1 900463 37 7
More Memories of Derby - 1 903204 20 8
Memories of Dewsbury & Batley - 1 900463 80 6
Memories of Doncaster - 1 900463 36 9
Nostalgic Dudley - 1 900463 03 2
Golden Years of Dudley - 1 903204 60 7
Memories of Edinburgh - 1 900463 33 4
Memories of Enfield - 1 903204 14 3
Memories of Exeter - 1 900463 94 6
Memories of Glasgow - 1 900463 68 7
More Memories of Glasgow - 1 903204 44 5
Memories of Gloucester - 1 903204 04 6
Memories of Grimsby - 1 900463 97 0
More Memories of Grimsby - 1 903204 36 4
Memories of Guildford - 1 903204 22 4
Memories of Halifax - 1 900463 05 9
More Memories of Halifax - 1 900463 06 7
Golden Years of Halifax - 1 900463 62 8
Nostalgic Halifax - 1 903204 30 5
Memories of Harrogate - 1 903204 01 1
Memories of Hartlepool - 1 900463 42 3
Memories of High Wycombe - 1 900463 84 9
Memories of Huddersfield - 1 900463 15 6
More Memories of Huddersfield - 1 900463 26 1
Golden Years of Huddersfield - 1 900463 77 6
Nostalgic Huddersfield - 1 903204 19 4
Huddersfield Town FC - 1 900463 51 2
Memories of Hull - 1 900463 86 5
More Memories of Hull - 1 903204 06 2
Hull Memories - 1 903204 70 4
Memories of Ipswich - 1 900463 09 1
More Memories of Ipswich - 1 903204 52 6
Memories of Keighley - 1 900463 01 6
Golden Years of Keighley - 1 900463 92 X

True North Books Ltd - Book List

Memories of Kingston - 1 903204 24 0
Memories of Leeds - 1 900463 75 X
More Memories of Leeds - 1 900463 12 1
Golden Years of Leeds - 1 903204 07 0
Memories of Leicester - 1 900463 08 3
More Memories of Leicester - 1 903204 08 9
Memories of Leigh - 1 903204 27 5
Memories of Lincoln - 1 900463 43 1
Memories of Liverpool - 1 900463 07 5
More Memories of Liverpool - 1 903204 09 7
Liverpool Memories - 1 903204 53 4
Memories of Luton - 1 900463 93 8
Memories of Macclesfield - 1 900463 28 8
Memories of Manchester - 1 900463 27 X
More Memories of Manchester - 1 903204 03 8
Manchester Memories - 1 903204 54 2
Memories of Middlesbrough - 1 900463 56 3
More Memories of Middlesbrough - 1 903204 42 9
Memories of Newbury - 1 900463 79 2
Memories of Newcastle - 1 900463 81 4
More Memories of Newcastle - 1 903204 10 0
Memories of Newport - 1 900463 59 8
Memories of Northampton - 1 900463 48 2
More Memories of Northampton - 1 903204 34 8
Memories of Norwich - 1 900463 73 3
Memories of Nottingham - 1 900463 91 1
More Memories of Nottingham - 1 903204 11 9
Bygone Oldham - 1 900463 25 3
Memories of Oldham - 1 900463 76 8
Memories of Oxford - 1 900463 54 7
Memories of Peterborough - 1 900463 98 9
Golden Years of Poole - 1 900463 69 5
Memories of Portsmouth - 1 900463 39 3
More Memories of Portsmouth - 1 903204 51 8
Nostalgic Preston - 1 900463 50 4
More Memories of Preston - 1 900463 17 2
Preston Memories - 1 903204 41 0
Memories of Reading - 1 900463 49 0
Memories of Rochdale - 1 900463 60 1
More Memories of Reading - 1 903204 39 9
More Memories of Rochdale - 1 900463 22 9
Memories of Romford - 1 903204 40 2
Memories of St Albans - 1 903204 23 2
Memories of St Helens - 1 900463 52 0
Memories of Sheffield - 1 900463 20 2
More Memories of Sheffield - 1 900463 32 6
Golden Years of Sheffield - 1 903204 13 5
Memories of Slough - 1 900 463 29 6
Golden Years of Solihull - 1 903204 55 0
Memories of Southampton - 1 900463 34 2
More Memories of Southampton - 1 903204 49 6
Memories of Stockport - 1 900463 55 5
More Memories of Stockport - 1 903204 18 6
Memories of Stockton - 1 900463 41 5
Memories of Stoke-on-Trent - 1 900463 47 4
More Memories of Stoke-on-Trent - 1 903204 12 7
Memories of Stourbridge - 1903204 31 3
Memories of Sunderland - 1 900463 71 7
More Memories of Sunderland - 1 903204 48 8
Memories of Swindon - 1 903204 00 3
Memories of Uxbridge - 1 900463 64 4
Memories of Wakefield - 1 900463 65 2
More Memories of Wakefield - 1 900463 89 X
Nostalgic Walsall - 1 900463 18 0
Golden Years of Walsall - 1 903204 56 9
More Memories of Warrington - 1 900463 02 4
Memories of Watford - 1 900463 24 5
Golden Years of West Bromwich - 1 900463 99 7
Memories of Wigan - 1 900463 85 7
Golden Years of Wigan - 1 900463 82 2
Nostalgic Wirral - 1 903204 15 1
Memories of Woking - 1 903204 32 1
Nostalgic Wolverhampton - 1 900463 53 9
Wolverhampton Memories - 1 903204 50 X
Memories of Worcester - 1 903204 25 9
Memories of Wrexham - 1 900463 23 7
Memories of York - 1 900463 66 0

Available in the Local Interest section of all major bookshops or direct from the publishers - telephone 01422 344344